MARGARET M. PEARSON

Discovering
London for Children

Revised by Jacqueline Fearn

D1825409

SHIRE PUBLICATIONS LTD

CONTENTS

Photographs are acknowledged as follows: R. D. Barrett-Lennard, plate 6; Eric de Mare/Gordon Fraser, plate 8; J. Garner, plate 7; Iris Hardwick, plate 10; Cadbury Lamb, plate 1; London Dungeon, plate 4; E. Preston, plates 2, 12; F. Spalding-Smith, plate 11; Victoria and Albert Museum, plate 5; R. Wilkinson-Latham, plate 9; G. N. Wright, plate 3. Line drawings by Edward Stamp.

Printed in Great Britain by C. I. Thomas & Sons (Haverfordwest) Ltd, Press Buildings, Merlins Bridge, Haverfordwest.

1. ROUND AND ABOUT BY BUS

More than 6,200 of the famous red buses ply up and down streets in London—and out of London—providing transport across some 630 square miles within a radius of about 15 miles from Charing Cross.

And if you want to take a comprehensive look at London, to get your bearings and see what you want to explore further, there is no better way than taking a Round London Sightseeing Tour. These start every hour on the hour from 10 a.m. till 9 p.m. (in winter till 4 p.m. only) every day except Christmas Day from Grosvenor Gardens near Victoria Station and from Piccadilly Circus and until 4 p.m. in summer and 2 p.m. in winter from Marble Arch.

It is best to go with someone who knows London, as there is no guide, though a free illustrated route diagram tells you what to look out for (and it is available in English, French, German, Spanish, Dutch and Italian).

The tour passes many of London's most famous places, including the Law Courts in Fleet Street, St. Paul's Cathedral, the Barbican development scheme in the City, the Monument, London Bridge, Tower Bridge, Westminster Abbey, Horse Guards Parade in Whitehall, Trafalgar Square, Buckingham Palace, Hyde Park Corner and Piccadilly Circus. In the evening many of the buildings are floodlit.

Where to make enquiries

London Transport enquiry offices (at Piccadilly Circus, Euston, Victoria, King's Cross, Oxford Circus and St. James's Park underground stations and the British Rail Travel Centre at Waterloo) supply free information leaflets, including the London Transport Official Tourist Information folded map showing tourist attractions and how to make the most of public transport.

The enquiry offices will also sell you Red Bus Rover tickets. They give you a day's unlimited travel over all the red bus routes, (ranging as far as St Albans and Leatherhead) and are also available from Underground stations and National Travel offices, between 9 a.m. and 5 p.m. Long stay visitors can try the 'Go-As-You-Please' Tourist Tickets which give you 4 or 7 days unlimited travel on all red buses and the entire Underground system (tickets from Underground stations and enquiry offices). A range of coach tours in and around London is offered throughout the year, from Victoria Coach Station. Obtain brochures from Victoria, enquiry offices or National Travel.

The red buses (like the Underground) come under the authority of the London Transport Executive.

If you have any travel enquiries, telephone 01-222 1234. There is a 24-hour service, and the answerers are very helpful.

Horses to Routemasters

The first regular bus service in London was begun in 1829 by George Shillibeer. His vehicles ran from Paddington Green to the Bank of England, and each was drawn by three horses.

Now, in an average working day, London's red buses carry over 4 million passengers. More than 75 per cent of the services are operated by double-deck vehicles mostly with a two-man crew, but one-man buses—called Red Arrows—have been introduced to provide a quick and frequent service in central London, linking the main shopping and entertainment areas with the main line railway stations. They carry 25 seated passengers (at the rear) and 48 standing. Passengers pay a flat rate as they enter, and leave through power-operated doors under the control of the driver.

There are several other types of bus running in London. Some of them are known as RTs, but they are gradually being withdrawn; their successor is the RM (Routemaster), of which there are now 2,561 in service. The standard RMs are 27 ft. 7 in. long and 8 ft. wide, and seat 64 passengers. They have now been superseded by 30 ft. long Routemasters (RML), which will seat 72, and more recently by the DMS 'Londoner' bus, which is one-man operated and carries 89 passengers (68 seated and 21 standing).

Trafalgar Square is served by more buses than any other place in London. More than 500 buses an hour are scheduled to pass through at peak periods.

Yards of ticket

Visitors to London are often intrigued by the red bus ticket machines, which, if you are buying long-run tickets for a family, will churn out a yard or so of paper. The machine most widely used is the Gibson (called after the inventor), which prints tickets from a blank roll of paper at the turn of a handle.

Far afield

London's red buses are famous all over the world. They have been on official tours of many countries, and they are sometimes sold overseas. Probably the most famous red buses *not* running in London are the six used to carry sightseers to Niagara Falls.

2. THE UNDERGROUND

Beneath London and its suburbs runs one of the largest electric underground systems in the world. It goes in all directions, and covers such a wide area that when the outskirts are reached, it comes up to ground level and operates as an ordinary surface railway. From Mondays to Fridays more than 2 million passenger journeys are made daily on this vast system, popularly known as the Underground.

There are basically two types of tunnels: 'cut and cover', constructed by digging a deep trench for the railway and then covering it over, and 'tube', constructed by boring through the ground from underground working sites. Over 250 route miles are run by the Underground; 99 of these are in tunnel—77 in 'tube' and 22 in 'cut and cover'.

The first sub-surface steam railway, which was nearly four miles long, was opened in 1863 and ran between Paddington and Farringdon Street. The newest complete Underground 'line' is the Victoria Line, which links Brixton, Victoria and the West End with the main railway stations at Euston, King's Cross and St. Pancras, and with the densely populated north-eastern suburbs. This was opened by the Queen in 1969. The extension of the Piccadilly Line to Heathrow Central opened in 1977 and the Jubilee Line, under construction from Baker Street to Charing Cross, is expected to open in 1978.

Central Tube Rover Tickets are available which entitle you to unlimited travel between any of the 49 stations on or inside the Circle Line and some important ones outside, taking you within easy reach of most major attractions. Any station in the Central area or an enquiry office will supply tickets.

Facts and curiosities

Escalators capable of carrying 9,000 passengers an hour in either direction at speeds of 92 to 145 ft. per minute are installed at 70 stations. The longest escalator is at Leicester Square—161 ft. 6 in. on a slope with a vertical rise of 80 ft. 9 in. The station with the most escalators is Oxford Circus, with 14.

In Bayswater, at 23 and 24 Leinster Gardens, dummy housefronts were built to preserve the street frontage when the Circle Line was cut close to the road.

A river flows above the platforms of Sloane Square underground station. An iron aqueduct carries the Westbourne, which flows from Hampstead to the Thames, via the Serpentine.

The busiest underground stations are Victoria, Oxford Circus, King's Cross, Piccadilly Circus, Waterloo and Liverpool Street.

---

3. ROUND TRIP ON THE RIVER

Frequent trips run from Westminster Pier both up and down the river from Easter or Whitsun. Some of the launches go up river as far as Hampton Court, and as far down river as Greenwich, where the *Cutty Sark* and *Gipsy Moth IV* are in permanent dry dock. Perhaps the most popular river excursion is a round trip from Westminster Pier down to Tower Bridge and back; a trip taking well under an hour.

Why 'Big Ben'?

Westminster Pier is reached by steps leading down to the quay from near the bronze statue of Boadicea in her chariot, near Big Ben and at the end of Westminster Bridge (which was built about 100 years ago).

Big Ben, by the way, is a bell, not a clock, though the clock, the chimes and even the tower itself are affectionately, if incorrectly, all thought of as Big Ben. It may have been called Big Ben after Sir Benjamin Hall, then First Commissioner of Works, or after a popular prize fighter, Benjamin Caunt. They were both 'big' enough; they each weighed 17 stone. Big Ben itself was cast at the Whitechapel Foundry in 1858. It has been in the belfry ever since. Each of the four faces of the clock is 23 ft. in diameter, and even the minute spaces are a foot square.

As you head by boat towards Tower Bridge, old **Scotland Yard** is on the left, in red brick and Portland stone. (In 1967, Scotland Yard moved to a huge new building in Broadway, off Victoria Street.)

A little further along the Embankment is the gilded bronze eagle **memorial to the R.A.F.,** unveiled in 1923.

Straight ahead is **Hungerford Bridge,** which carries the main railway line across the river from Charing Cross Station. It is not a glamorous bridge, and the foot bridge is definitely unattractive, but it gives a wonderful view, particularly at night, of St. Paul's, the Royal Festival Hall, and the lights of London reflected in the dark water.

Next landmark on the left is **Cleopatra's Needle** (see page 74), round which Moses is said to have played as a boy. Behind the Embankment Gardens is Shell-Mex House and the Savoy Hotel.

The next bridge is **Waterloo Bridge,** the second of its name, and well worth walking across one day to see the fine view both upstream and down (and the swans paddling about on the muddy banks when the tide is out).

'Somerset had his head cut off'

Then comes the famous **Somerset House,** with its 600 ft. facade facing the Thames. It was for many years the home of the Registry of Births, Marriages and Deaths; and here wills were deposited, among them those of Shakespeare, Van Dyck, Isaac Newton and John Milton. (The Registry is now at St Catherine's House, Aldwych.) The building occupies the site of the princely palace begun by Edward Seymour, Lord Protector Somerset, uncle of the child-king Edward VI, whose mother Jane Seymour (third wife of Henry VIII) died shortly after his birth. Somerset was one of the regents appointed to rule England during Edward's minority, but he was outwitted by more ruthless rivals and executed in 1522, wearing for the occasion a splendid costume fine enough for a State banquet. (The unfeeling young king, to whom his uncle had always been kind, entered in his journal the terse comment: 'Somerset had his head cut off'.) Elizabeth lived for a time at Somerset House while her sister was on the throne, and Oliver Cromwell lay in state there for five weeks while preparations were made for his funeral.

Moored by the Embankment near Somerset House and the Temple Gardens are a river police station; the *Discovery,* the ship which carried Captain Scott on his Antarctic Expedition in 1901-1905; the *Wellington,* which serves as the Livery Hall of the Master Mariners' Company; and two training ships used by the London Division of the Royal Naval Volunteer Reserve—H.M.S. *Chrysanthemum* and *President.*

The tallest Wren steeple

Just before reaching **Blackfriars Bridge** you can glimpse the three-tiered 'wedding-cake' spire of **St. Bride's church,** the tallest of all Wren's steeples. Samuel Pepys was born nearby and was christened in the old church, where Richard Lovelace, the Cavalier poet, was buried. It was Lovelace who wrote the famous lines: *Stone walls do not a prison make, Nor iron bars a cage.*

Blackfriars Bridge takes its name from the black habits of the Dominican friars whose priory backed on to the Thames. Their Great Hall was the scene of the trial of Katherine of Aragon (held before Cardinal Wolsey) when Henry VIII was seeking a divorce in order to marry Anne Boleyn.

Just past Blackfriars Bridge is the Mermaid Theatre — the first theatre built in the City since the days of the Puritans. The theatre was built in Puddle Dock, where a Roman boat was found in 1962.

7

Away on the left is **St. Paul's Cathedral,** and just before South-wark Bridge you can see the spire of another Wren church—**St. James Garlickhithe.** The derivation of this word is interesting. It was a district where many Italians settled, who ate and sold—garlic.

Old London Bridge

After passing under Southwark Bridge and Cannon Street Railway Bridge, we come to **London Bridge,** which thousands of people cross every day, flooding the City with workers in the morning, and draining it almost empty as they leave in the evening. The famous Old London Bridge stood a few hundred yards to the east of the present bridge. There were various early wooden bridges over the river, but the most famous bridge of all was the stone bridge built by Peter, Chaplain of St. Mary Colechurch; not so unlikely a man as might be supposed, as the church had from early days encouraged bridge building as an act of piety. The stone for Peter's bridge was mainly Kentish Rag. It was begun in 1176, finished in 1209, and remained the *only* bridge over the tidal Thames till 1739. It stood on 19 great supports with a spiked drawbridge in the southern half. The heads (and sometimes the quarters) of executed people were often stuck on the spikes till they rotted and fell off. Houses, shops and a chapel (to St. Thomas a Becket) were built on the bridge, the rents from the houses and shops going towards the cost of the upkeep. This wonderful old bridge was finally demolished—with much regret on all sides—only after the completion of John Rennie's bridge in 1831.

Rennie's bridge has now been demolished piecemeal, and rebuilt at the same time. This work was begun at the end of 1967. The new bridge carries six lanes of traffic. Rennie's bridge has been reconstructed in Arizona, U.S.A.

That part of the Thames that is downstream from London Bridge is called the Port of London, upstream is the King's Reach, while immediately downstream is the famous Pool of London.

Just past London Bridge you will see the top of **The Monument** and smell (perhaps) **Billingsgate,** London's big fish market. Billingsgate Wharf is probably the oldest on the river; it has been used by fishermen ever since the ninth century. Billingsgate takes its name from an old gate called after Belin, a legendary king of the Britons. It claims to be the only market in the world where every kind of fish is sold—'wet, dry and shell'.

Traitor's Gate

Next comes **All Hallows by-the-Tower** (see page 32), and then we pass the **Tower of London** (and the Traitor's Gate) and finally reach **Tower Bridge**, the most famous and picturesque bridge across the Thames today. The 800 ft. span between the Gothic towers of the bridge can be raised in two parts to let ships pass up and down the river. The two drawbridges weigh 1,000 tons each, but they can be raised (by hydraulic machinery) in 1½ minutes (see plate 2).

Going back towards Westminster Pier we pass on the left warehouses and wharves. At the southern end of London Bridge is **Southwark Cathedral,** a much-restored medieval church — possibly the finest Gothic building in London after West- minster Abbey. There is a chapel in the cathedral called after John Harvard, founder of Harvard University in Massachusetts in the United States. He was the son of a Southwark butcher and was christened in the church in 1607. Shakespeare's younger brother, Edmund, who died the same year, is buried in the cathedral. Southwark is a district Shakespeare knew well. The Globe Theatre was built by his friends the Burbages in 1599, and he acted there and had 15 of his plays produced there.

Someone on the launch will probably point out a seventeenth century house from which Sir Christopher Wren is said to have watched the building of St. Paul's (which is almost directly op- posite). But there is no evidence that Wren ever lived there, or that he annoyed his wife by rushing to the window without even waiting to put on his wig!

The largest offices in Europe

Under Blackfriars and Waterloo Bridges again, and on the left is the **Royal Festival Hall,** whose auditorium seats 3,000. At the back you can see the two big blocks of **Shell Centre** (linked by a tunnel). The blocks cover 7½ acres, and are said to be the largest offices in Europe. They were completed in 1962.

The last big building before returning to Westminster Pier is **County Hall,** 750 ft. long, the headquarters of the Greater London Council which (apart from the City, which governs itself) rules such things as ambulance and fire services, health and welfare, drainage, libraries, and major roads in Greater London.

As the launch turns you can see **St. Thomas's Hospital** on the left, and directly opposite the **Houses of Parliament,** which in- corporate the magnificent old Westminster Hall. The tallest tower is the Victoria Tower, 336 ft. high and 75 ft. square—the tallest square tower in the world. A flag flies from this tower during the day if Parliament is sitting. If it is sitting at night, a light shines in the Clock Tower.

During the summer only, you can telephone Westminster Pier and enquire about the trips from 01-930 8294, or 01-930 2074. Or ask about river trips (and other excursions) at the London Tourist Board which has information centres at 26, Grosvenor Gardens, near Victoria Station (01-730 0791), Selfridges, Harrods and the Tower.

The longest rowing race in the world is the Doggett's Coat and Badge Race, instituted by Thomas Doggett, a well-known actor-manager, in 1716, in honour of George I's accession. Six Thames Watermen compete in the final, at the end of July, rowing about five miles from London Bridge to Chelsea. The champion wins an orange coat with a large silver badge on the left sleeve, representing the White Horse of Hanover (plate 6).

4. WESTMINSTER ABBEY

Westminster Abbey is such an enormous place (513 ft long), with so much to see, that it is easiest to explore if you divide it into three—Edward the Confessor's Shrine, Henry VII's Chapel, and the Abbey of the 'commoners'.

The 'commoners' Abbey is itself divided (very roughly) into different areas for different types of people. By tradition, great soldiers, sailors and explorers are buried in the Nave; poets and writers around Chaucer in Poets' Corner in the South Transept (on the right of the nave); statesmen round William Pitt and Gladstone in the North Transept; musicians around Henry Purcell in the north aisle of the Choir, and scientists around Sir Isaac Newton near the Choir Screen.

Prime interest in the Abbey is always centred in Edward the Confessor's Shrine, commemorating the founder of the church, and in Henry VII's magnificent chapel, built as his own resting place and for the burial of other sovereigns who came after him. There is an admission charge for the royal chapels, transepts and Choir. Last tickets sold, Monday to Friday, 4 p.m. and Saturday 5 p.m. (closed between 2 p.m. and 3.45 p.m.).

The first Norman building in England

When London was the chief town of the small kingdom of Essex, King Sebert of Essex built the first church of St. Peter on Thorney Island, a marshy island formed by two streams flowing into the Thames.

This building was largely destroyed by the Danes, and **Edward the Confessor,** who had a special affection for St. Peter, founded the church as we know it today. Its official name is 'the Collegiate Church of St. Peter in Westminster'.

Edward, with his brilliant eyes and long white hair, was much revered by his subjects. His abbey was almost as large as the present building, except for Henry VII's Chapel. Edward had been brought up in Normandy and was fond of both that country and its people, so the church, under his guidance, became the first Norman structure in England. It was finished at Christmas time, 1065.

In the first week of 1066 Edward died and was buried in the Abbey. King Harold was killed at Hastings, and on Christmas Day **William the Conqueror** was crowned in the Abbey. William, like Edward, created a precedent—Edward by being buried in the Abbey, William by being crowned there. Up to the time of George II, all but a handful of our sovereigns were buried in the Abbey, and all but two—Edward V and Edward VIII—have been crowned there. William is not buried in the Abbey, but perhaps King Sebert is. The tomb thought to be his is by the gates of the South Ambulatory.

The king who closed the shops of London

Edward the Confessor's church was very largely rebuilt by Henry III (King John's son), who wanted to honour the memory and the remains of the saintly Edward. **Henry III** (1216-1272) was a pious spendthrift. He had a genuine appreciation for art, and wanted to build something for London that would rival the beauties of Rheims and Amiens. He raised the money in various ways. Having 'persuaded' a Jewish widow to present £2,500 to his rebuilding fund, he impulsively had all his children weighed—and their weight in gold given to the poor. He instituted a fair in Tothill Fields near Westminster Abbey to raise money for his project and commanded all shops in London to close for 15 days, so that the fair would make more money for the building fund. (But it rained and rained, and the people in London suffered 'pitifullie in mire and durt'.) He got into such financial difficulties that he and his wife, Eleanor of Provence, had to invite themselves out to dine with London's wealthy merchants. In 1267, he pawned the jewels he had collected for Edward the Confessor's Shrine. However, he promised to restore them within 18 months — and he did. He was so pious that during a visit to France he insisted on saying a mass at every church he passed. This so annoyed the French king that he ordered every church on the way to Paris to close as the royal procession approached.

In 1269, the new building was consecrated, and Edward the Confessor's body was placed in the magnificent new shrine.

11

EDWARD THE CONFESSOR'S SHRINE

As time went by, other sovereigns were buried in the Confessor's Shrine. They were (from the left as you walk round) Queen Philippa and her husband Edward III, Richard II and Anne of Bohemia, Edward I, Queen Maud, wife of Henry I, Queen Editha, wife of the Confessor, Henry III, and Queen Eleanor (Edward I's wife). Henry V is buried beneath his own Chantry Chapel at the entrance to the Confessor's Shrine.

Henry III died in 1272, and was buried in a splendid tomb, once studded with jewels and glass mosaic. But his heart (as he had promised) was sent to the Abbey of Fontevrault in France, where Richard Coeur de Lion and his grandfather Henry II were buried.

An heroic queen and a boy king who lost his slipper

Queen Eleanor of Castile died in 1290. She had been Edward I's constant companion throughout their married life, even accompanying him on Crusades. She was a greatly loved woman, for her courage in sucking poison from a wound when Edward was attacked by an assassin in the Holy Land, for her kindness to the poor, and for her loving care of her seven surviving daughters and one surviving son. An anniversary memorial service was held at her tomb for at least 250 years, with 100 candles burning and all the bells clanging.

Queen Philippa of Hainault and her husband **Edward III** (died 1377) were the parents of twelve children, including the Black Prince. **Richard II** was the son of the Black Prince. Richard, who was only ten when he succeeded his grandfather, fainted during the long Coronation service. Knights cleared a way for him, and as he was carried out of the Abbey to the Palace of Westminister, through the surging crowd, he lost 'one of the blessed slippers of the regalia'. When he grew up, Richard replaced the lost slipper with a pair of velvet shoes. Richard's **Queen Anne** (of Bohemia) died of the plague. He was later murdered at Pontefract Castle, and buried obscurely at King's Langley. After persistent rumours that he was alive, Henry V had his body exhumed. He adorned the corpse with royal robes, and himself followed Richard's second funeral as chief mourner. This time Richard was buried in the Abbey, and now shares a double tomb with his much-loved Anne.

Three chargers at the high altar

Henry V, a popular hero after the battle of Agincourt, and a generous benefactor to the Abbey, was given one of the most impressive funerals the Abbey has ever witnessed. The king died in 1422 (probably of dysentery) aged 33, while campaigning in France. His black-hung, sombre funeral procession wound its way some 250 miles from Vincennes to Paris, across the Channel from Calais to Dover, and up to London, where his leather funeral effigy was met by all the bishops in England. Clergy chanted unceasingly as they followed with 1,400 lighted tapers. Behind the bier came Henry's attractive young wife, Catherine de Valois. When the procession reached the Abbey, Henry's three chargers were led right up to the High Altar. They carried his armour. His helmet, saddle and shield are on view on a beam over his tomb. The effigy on his tomb had been carved in his own lifetime of solid oak, with his head and hands made of silver. In Henry VIII's reign the silver was stolen and Henry V was headless till 1972 when he was given a head and hands of polyester resin.

Pepys visits royalty

When **Catherine de Valois** (the wife of Henry V and Owen Tudor) died in 1437, she was buried with great pomp in the Lady Chapel. Henry VII pulled this chapel down when building his own, and Catherine's body was eventually placed in a coffin of loose boards by Henry V's tomb. The vergers of the day for a shilling a time would take off the lid to allow visitors to see the royal remains. Samuel Pepys went one better. In 1669, he wrote that he saw...'the body of Queen Catherine of Valois, and I had the upper part of her body in my hands, and I did kiss her mouth, reflecting upon it that I did kiss a Queene, and that this was my birthday 36 years old that I did kiss a Queene'. Catherine was finally buried under the altar slab in Henry V's Chantry Chapel.

The Coronation Chair

At the far end of the Confessor's Shrine is the somewhat battered Coronation Chair, made for Edward I. Under its seat is the famous Stone of Scone, upon which Scottish kings were crowned for hundreds of years. Edward brought it to London after he had defeated the Scots in 1297. For Coronation ceremonies, the chair is placed in the Sanctuary (the space between the altar rails). The only times the chair has left the Abbey were when Cromwell had it taken to Westminster Hall for his installation as Lord Protector, and when it was taken away for safety during the two World Wars.

HENRY VII'S CHAPEL

The main part of the Abbey as we know it was the work of Henry III, carried out during twenty-five years, but the completed church is the work of various kings (and abbots) over five centuries.

Henry VII was the other great royal builder. His magnificent chapel, one of the glories of England, completely transformed the eastern end of the Abbey. The handsome gates to the chapel are of oak and bronze, divided into open panels, and decorated with heraldic devices to commemorate the fact that the marriage of Henry VII (a Lancastrian) to Elizabeth (of York) finally ended the

Wars of the Roses. The falcon represents Elizabeth's father, Edward IV, the daisy and portcullis make a punning reference to Henry's mother, Margaret Beaufort, the leopards represent England, and a crown and double roses on a thorn bush recall Henry's own hasty first coronation on the battlefield when Richard III was killed at Bosworth.

These gates lead to the double row of seats for the Knights of the Bath, which run along both sides of the nave of the chapel. Each stall has a tip-up seat, carved with strange creatures — pigs and dragons, a mermaid and her comb, a jester, three monkeys and a cooking pot, and the devil himself, playing a drum.

Seventy kings, queens, princes and princesses

In Henry VII's Chapel some seventy kings and queens, princes and princesses lie under the bright silk banners of the Knights of the Bath and under the delicate fan tracery of the exquisite roof. Henry himself died in 1509, about ten years before the building was completed. He was buried where he had planned to be buried, with his wife. Their tomb is shared by **James I** (died 1625), who has no memorial. Under the altar lies the young Tudor king, **Edward VI,** who died of consumption at the age of 15 in 1553.

Two sisters and 'the little princes in the Tower'

There are two important chapels in the North and South Aisles of Henry VII's Chapel. The entrances are clearly marked on either side of the gates.

In North Aisle is the **Queen Elizabeth Chapel.** Here the coffin of the great Tudor queen (died 1603) lies on top of that of her half-sister, 'Bloody' Mary (died 1558). **Mary** had no memorial at all till James I had a Latin epitaph inscribed on the tomb: *Consorts both in throne and grave, here rest two sisters, in the hope of one resurrection.*

This chapel has sometimes been called the Chapel of the Innocents. In it are buried the 'little princes in the Tower'—twelve-year-old **Edward V** and his eight-year-old brother Richard, murdered together in 1483. The tomb was designed by Christopher Wren at the request of Charles II. Here, too, lie two little daughters of James I—the baby Princess Sophia in her coloured alabaster cradle and coverlet (one of the most charming memorials to be seen anywhere) and, in stomacher and Medici collar, her two-year-old sister Mary. Watched over by her nurses, the little girl murmured 'I go...I go...Away I go!'

Mary, Queen of Scots, and Queen Anne's eighteen children

Opposite Queen Elizabeth's Chapel in the South Aisle is the Lady Margaret Chapel, where **Margaret Beaufort, Countess of Richmond,** mother of Henry VII, is buried, in one of the most beautiful of all the Abbey monuments. She was the founder of Christ's and St. John's Colleges, Cambridge.

In the same chapel is a memorial to **Margaret Douglas, Countess of Lennox,** the mother of Lord Darnley, whose marriage to Mary, Queen of Scots, proved so disastrous. (She was thus the grandmother of James VI of Scotland—James I of England.) One of the figures kneeling on this tomb is Darnley himself.

Mary, Queen of Scots, lies in a fine tomb decorated with Scottish thistles. After her execution in 1587 she was buried in Peterborough Cathedral, but 25 years later her son James I had her reburied in the Abbey.

In this aisle also are buried **Charles II** (died 1685) and **William and Mary** (William died in 1702, following an accident when his horse stumbled over a molehill; Mary died in 1694).

Queen Anne (died 1714) and her husband are also buried in the Lady Margaret Chapel with their 18 children. One boy lived to be ten. The others were all stillborn or died in infancy.

The Battle of Britain

Henry VII's Chapel was the last of the royal additions and alterations to the Abbey, but the very end of the chapel—the east end of the Abbey—has been made into a special R.A.F. Battle of Britain Remembrance Chapel.

The windows here contain the badges of 63 Fighter Squadrons which took part in the Battle of Britain, and above the badges are the flags of the Dominions and Allies whose men were amongst those killed. At the foot of the windows are Shakespeare's words, spoken by Henry V: *We few, we happy few, we band of brothers.*

THE COMMONERS' ABBEY

Churchill

Having explored Edward the Confessor's Shrine and Henry VII's Chapel, there is still the rest of the Abbey to be seen.

Only a few steps inside the West Door is a green marble slab saying simply: *Remember Winston Churchill. In accordance with the wishes of the Queen and Parliament, the Dean and Chapter placed this stone on 25th anniversary of the Battle of Britain, 15th September, 1965.*

Churchill spoke of the valiant, outnumbered Battle of Britain fighter pilots, the famous words:"Never in the field of human conflict was so much owed by so many to so few". He died in 1965, and is buried in the country churchyard of Bladon, near Blenheim Palace, in Oxfordshire, where he was born.

A body picked at random

A few steps further on is the grave of **the Unknown Warrior.** The idea of burying an unknown soldier was suggested by the Rev. David Railton, M.C., a chaplain in the First World War. He saw a grave in France with the pencilled inscription: 'An unknown soldier of the Black Watch'. The British government approved the idea. The bodies of four men killed in the main battle areas of France—the Aisne, the Somme, Arras and Ypres— were placed in a chapel. Each man was covered with a Union Jack, and one was picked at random by the general officer in charge of troops in France and Flanders. He was brought to England and given the funeral of a king on Armistice Day, November 11th, 1920. The procession was headed by King George V, and as the coffin reached the Abbey, it passed through two lines of holders of the Victoria Cross. The body was buried in earth brought from France under a marble slab quarried in Belgium. Nearby, on a pillar, hangs the American Congressional Medal, bestowed on the Unknown Warrior by the government of the United States of America.

Murdered for his ring

Tombs and memorials are thick along the walls of the Abbey. Many of the people honoured are now forgotten, but sometimes men who are at least half-forgotten come into the news again.

One such man is **Admiral Sir Cloudesley Shovel,** whose tomb is in the South Aisle (which leads to Poets' Corner). Until a few years ago most people would have passed his monument without a second glance. But in 1968 and 1969, divers off the Isles of Scilly discovered the wreck of the *Association* and other ships that foundered there in 1707 when returning to England after a battle with the French. The ships lost their bearings in bad weather, and the *Association,* carrying Shovel's flag, struck the Western Rocks, and broke up. Shovel was washed ashore, but was murdered by a woman for a ring he was wearing.

The poet who was buried standing up

Poet's Corner was first mentioned as such by Oliver Goldsmith (who is remembered here but is buried in the Temple churchyard). The principal tomb (against the wall on the right) is that of **Geoffrey Chaucer** (died 1400), author of *The Canterbury Tales.* Also buried in Poets' Corner are Edmund Spenser (died 1599), author of *The Faerie Queene,* Charles Dickens, Tennyson, Browning, Hardy and Kipling. There are memorials to Longfellow, as a tribute to American poetry, to the Bronte sisters, to Shakespeare, Keats, Shelley, Robert Burns and John Milton. **Ben Jonson** (died 1637) comes off best. He has a memorial in Poets' Corner—and is buried in the Nave. There are various stories about Jonson, who was born in the neighbourhood and educated at Westminster School. He was a friend of Shakespeare and tutor to Sir Walter Raleigh's son. He is said to have asked Charles I a favour—for 18 square inches of ground. "Where?" asked the king. "In Westminster Abbey!" came the answer — and he was buried in the Abbey, standing up. (Nearby is **David Livingstone,** the African explorer and missionary, who is buried under a large white slab let into the stone on the north side of the Nave. He died in the centre of Africa in 1873.)

He lived for 150 years

History seems eternal when you go through the Abbey. So does life itself if you look at a small memorial in the floor in Poets' Corner—to **Thomas Parr,** a farm servant from Salop. He lived on and on, remarried at 120, had a child, and finally called it quits when he was 150. He lived from 1485 to 1635—through the reigns of Richard III, Henry VII, Henry VIII and his three children Edward VI, Mary and Elizabeth, James I and Charles I, who entertained him so royally that perhaps he helped the old man on his way to Paradise!

Dick Whittington and his cat

Very little of the ancient glass is left in Westminster Abbey. Some was deliberately destroyed by the Puritans, some was broken during rebuilding and restoration work, and some was destroyed during the Second World War. But on the north side of the Nave (on the left as you enter by the West Door) is a series of windows designed and carried out by Sir Ninian Comper, R.A., between 1907 and 1961. Each window embodies figures of the kings and abbots in whose reign the Nave was gradually built—and incorporates legends or incidents connected with them.

Thus Edward the Confessor is shown with the Charter of the Foundation of the Abbey, and he is holding up the ring which, according to legend, he gave to St. John the Evangelist, who appeared to him disguised as a beggar. Other kings shown in these windows are Henry III, Henry V (with a small picture at the bottom left-hand corner of his great Mayor of London — Dick Whittington—and his cat, a marmalade one), Richard II, Edward III and Edward I. A scene in this window shows Henry III's heart being handed over to the abbess of Fontevrault.

The 'flogging headmaster'

The black and white pavement in the Choir was presented by **Dr. Richard Busby,** the 'flogging headmaster' of Westminster

17

School both during the Commonwealth (though he made no secret of his royalist sympathies) and after the Restoration. In spite of his respect for royalty, he refused to remove his cap in the presence of Charles II. "If I did," he said "the boys would think you more important than I". He died in 1695 and is buried beneath his black and white pavement.

---

5. EXHIBITION OF ABBEY TREASURES

We have read in the previous chapter that for over 900 years sovereigns have been crowned and buried in Westminster Abbey. It was once the custom to place life-sized effigies of sovereigns and other famous people on their coffins at their funerals. After the funeral, the effigy would lie in state, and then eventually be stored in a loft above Henry V's Chantry.

Many of the Westminster Abbey effigies have just crumbled away and been lost, but a dozen or so are on show in the Exhibition of Abbey Treasures in the Norman Undercroft in the Cloisters. The oldest are of wood, hay and plaster. Later ones were made of wax. The Exhibition is small and compact and needs no guide book.

A left-handed king

Just by the entrance is an enlarged section of the Bayeux Tapestry, showing (in Edward the Confessor's funeral) the only contemporary picture of Westminster Abbey. Nearby lies the oldest funeral effigy in Europe—that of **Edward III,** the victor of Crecy. His face, of wood, shows his mouth and left-hand cheek affected by the stroke that killed him in 1377. Doctors who examined the effigy when it was restored some years ago decided that Edward was left-handed. He was, nevertheless, noted for his fine penmanship. Edward was a handsome man, and during restoration, some of his hair was found—still reddish-gold. (The hair was analysed by forensic laboratory experts at Scotland Yard. They found that the effigy's eyebrows were made of dog's hair!)

Next is the funeral effigy of **Anne of Bohemia,** who died of the plague in 1394, leaving her king Richard II disconsolate. (For a year after her death, he refused to enter any door they had entered together.) Though Anne's head is of oak, it was carved from a death mask attributed to one Roger Elys, a tallow chandler in

London, noted for his waxworks at the end of the fourteenth century. Some of Anne's hair was caught in a nail driven into the oaken head. It was brown. Alongside Anne is a magnificent book, *Liber Regalis,* the book of the coronation, beautifully printed in red and black lettering and richly illuminated at the command of Richard II. It was used at Anne's coronation and since then has been used at every coronation in Westminster Abbey.

The sword of Henry V

Another fine effigy is that of **Catherine de Valois,** the attractive wife of Henry V, and later of Owen Tudor, founder of the great Tudor dynasty. Near her is a special display of the funeral armour of Henry V, including what is probably the oldest saddle in Europe, and the sword Henry used at the battle of Agincourt.

The most striking exhibit in the Exhibition is the death mask of **Henry VII.** This mask (made in 1509) reveals every detail of his bone structure and features—the determined, slightly humorous mouth, the firm nose and observant eyes. Small tufts of hair, red turning to grey, have been found round the ears.

The playing-card queen

Sharing the same glass case is the effigy of Henry's queen, **Elizabeth of York,** a broad, well-covered face. She is said to be the queen in all four suits of playing cards made in England. The first pack was made in England about 1487. She died in 1503. She was related to no fewer than ten kings and queens—Edward IV (father), Edward V (brother), Richard III (uncle), Henry VII (husband), Henry VIII (son), and Edward VI (grandson). Mary Tudor and Elizabeth I were both her granddaughters, and her own daughters both married kings—Margaret becoming the wife of James IV of Scotland, and Mary marrying Louis XII of France.

A curiosity among the effigies is that of **General Monk,** a leader in the Cromwellian Army who was largely responsible for the restoration of Charles II. Monk's actual effigy is encased in full armour, and wears a fresh white neckerchief.

Next is the most famous of the effigies, that of **Charles II** — 'a tall dark man, above two yards high' (as he was described in a proclamation offering £1,000 for his betrayal after his escape from the battle of Worcester). The effigy is dressed in his own garter robes and cloth-of-silver doublet and breeches. He died in 1685, asking as he lay dying: "Open the curtains, that I may once more see the day" (plate 8).

19

The oldest stuffed bird in England

Next to him is Frances Stuart, later the **Duchess of Richmond and Lennox.** She was one of the many women whom Charles admired. She was generally considered a great beauty, and posed for the figure of Britannia on our old pennies. She died in 1702. Her little parrot, a favourite pet, died a few days later. It is exhibited with her—probably the oldest stuffed bird in England.

Catherine, Duchess of Buckingham (died 1743), is also there in effigy. She was the illegitimate daughter of James II by Catherine Sedley. James loved her deeply, but she said: "It cannot be for my beauty, because I haven't any, and it cannot be for my wit, because he hasn't enough to know I have any". The duchess, however, had little sense of humour, and took her royal blood very seriously, insisting that visitors should bow themselves out backwards. John Sheffield, first Duke of Buckingham (the Lord Chamberlain), was her second husband. He built the original house where Buckingham Palace now stands.

As well as effigies, there are several commemorative figures in the Exhibition. The most striking of these is **Lord Nelson,** who died at the battle of Trafalgar in 1805. He was buried in St. Paul's. This excellent model is dressed in his own clothes. Gieves, the tailor who made his uniform, and Lock's of St. James's, who made his cocked hat (with a green shade attached to cover his blind eye), are still in business in London.

Gift from a queen

The most romantic exhibit in the Exhibition is the gold and cameo ring Elizabeth I gave to her young favourite, **Robert Devereux, Earl of Essex,** telling him to send it to her if ever he were in peril. The time came when he was in deadly peril—under sentence of death in the Tower of London. He sent the ring to the queen, but court jealousy prevented it reaching her, and Essex was executed in 1601. This ring was once set (under glass) into Elizabeth's tomb in the Abbey, but after an attempt was made to prize it out of its setting in 1964, it was put into the Exhibition for safe keeping.

Also in the Exhibition are reproductions of the Crown Jewels used at coronation rehearsals and some models of the Queen's Beasts. The originals, 6 ft. tall, stood outside Westminster Abbey when Queen Elizabeth II was crowned on June 2nd, 1953. They are now at Hampton Court. Each of these beasts was the emblem of one of the royal families from which our present royal family is descended. They are the lion of England, the unicorn of Scotland, the falcon of the Plantagenets, the griffin of Edward III, the Welsh dragon and greyhound of the Tudors, the bull of Clarence, the white lion of Mortimer, the yale of the Beauforts, and the white horse of Hanover.

Admission

The museum is open every day except Sunday, 9.30 a.m. to 4 p.m. There is an admission charge.

---

6. TROOPING THE COLOUR AND CHANGING THE GUARD

Trooping the Colour is a military ceremony held on the sovereign's official birthday, which is always on a Saturday in June. It begins at 11 a.m. Two rehearsals are held on the previous two Saturdays and the ceremony itself will be postponed if the weather is too bad. The Guards' uniforms are so expensive they must not be allowed to become soaked.

'Colours' are ceremonial silk flags: consecrated symbolic emblems of a regiment's or battalion's traditions. They are held in high esteem and treated with great respect, always being carried by officers and guarded by colour-sergeants. Trooping the Colour originated in an old ceremony known as lodging the colour. This was performed at the end of the day and no soldier was allowed to dismiss until the colour had been lodged in the billet of the officer in charge of it.

In the expression Trooping the Colour, the word 'trooping' means marching to music, and the drill of the Guards performing the Trooping the Colour has made the ceremony world famous, and you must get to the Horse Guards Parade early if you are to have a chance of seeing it.

The ceremony is both long and complicated. Only after the men have fallen in under their officers is the colour handed over by the Regimental Sergeant-Major to the Ensign of the Escort. Then comes the actual trooping, when the colour is marched along the ranks so that every man can see it and recognise it. (This was, of course, a matter of great importance when colours were still carried in battle, as the flags were the rallying points for soldiers.)

The trooping is followed by the famous march past, in both slow and quick time, to the music of massed bands. The Queen takes the salute and then returns to Buckingham Palace (riding side-saddle on a well-schooled horse; sometimes it is a police horse, sometimes one of her own) at the head of her Guards.

The scarlet tunics and bearskins are common to the Brigade of Guards as a whole.

Each regiment has distinguishing features of uniform:

Regiment	Hatband	Bearskin	Buttons
Grenadier	Scarlet	White goat - hair plume on left	Set singly
Coldstream	White	Scarlet plume on right	Set in pairs
Scots	Red, white and green diced	No plume	Set in threes
Irish	Green	Pale blue feather plume on right	Set in fours
Welsh	Black	White and green plume on left	Set in fives

Admission

Seating for both the rehearsals and the actual Trooping is balloted for, and applications for tickets (two only for each applicant) must be made to the Brigade Major, Household Division, Horse Guards, Whitehall, London, S.W.1, before March 1st each year. Tickets for the first rehearsal are free. There is a charge for tickets for the second rehearsal and for the Trooping itself (telephone 01-930 4466 for current prices) with no reduction for children. Standing room is free down the approach road, but it is a question of arriving early enough to see what is going on. There is always a huge crowd.

The Changing of the Guard

Horse Guards Parade, where the Trooping is held, is on the site of the old tilt-yard of Whitehall Palace. An archway leads from the parade ground to the courtyard where mounted sentries of the Queen's Life Guard are relieved every hour—and where the Changing of the Guard takes place every day at 11 a.m. (except on Sundays, when it is held at 10 a.m.). The ceremony takes about half an hour. It is colourful and photogenic, so there is always a crowd in the very limited space. The Queen's Life Guard, mounted on black horses, is provided by the Household Cavalry.

Everyone may *walk* through the archway—but only the Queen and a very few privileged people are allowed to *drive* through.

There is another Guard changing ceremony, that of the Queen's Guard at Buckingham Palace where, daily from April to early autumn, every other day during the winter months, the Guard is changed in the yard in front of the Palace. The new guard marches behind a band from either Wellington or Chelsea Barracks, and arrives in the forecourt at about 11.30 a.m. This ceremony also lasts about half an hour. When the Court is in London, the Queen's Colour of crimson is carried. Otherwise the Regimental Colour, based on the Union Jack, is carried. In very bad weather, the formal ceremony is cancelled.

How to get there

Horse Guards Parade is a few minutes' walk from Trafalgar Square underground station and from all the buses that pass through the square.

Buckingham Palace is near St. James's, Victoria or Green Park underground stations. No buses pass Buckingham Palace, but it is only a short walk from Hyde Park Corner.

7. THE ROYAL MEWS

What looks like the entrance to the Royal Mews behind Buckingham Palace—a gateway topped on each side with a lion and a unicorn—is really the exit.

The entrance is an ordinary doorway a few yards further down Buckingham Palace Road on the left. Turnstiles let you into a big quadrangle where the lamps are topped with golden crowns. Carriages, coaches, harness and the horses themselves occupy buildings on all four sides of the square.

Chief attraction is the **Gold State Coach,** used for every coronation since that of George IV. When it was made in 1762 for George III, it was described as 'very superb'. It is still very superb. It is 24 ft. long, 8 ft. 3 ins. wide, 12 ft. high, and gilded all over.

The lavishly decorated framework of the coach consists of eight palm trees which branch out at the top to support the roof. There are all kinds of symbolic decorations, including, at the very top, three cherubs supporting the Royal Crown and holding the Sceptre, the Sword of State and the Ensign of Knighthood. It is drawn by eight postillion horses, and can proceed only at walking speed.

In the **State Carriage House** on the right at the end of the square are many other handsome coaches, including the Glass State Coach used for all royal weddings since the time of George V's coronation. It generally carries the bride and bridegroom from the church, as it did when the Queen (then Princess Elizabeth) married the Duke of Edinburgh.

Another coach here is Queen Alexandra's State Coach. She and Edward VII used it to attend operas, balls and banquets. It is often seen in London still, as it carries new ambassadors to Buckingham Palace to present their credentials to the Queen. It has also been used, with a cushion on a specially installed table, to carry the Imperial State Crown to the House of Lords for the opening of Parliament.

As you leave the State Carriage House, the sweet smell of hay directs you to the adjoining **stables.** On one side stand the greys—the Windsor Greys, their tails bound in pale blue; on the other are the bays—predominantly Cleveland Bays with their tails bound in red. The Windsor Greys are not a special breed. Until George V began using them in London, they were employed mainly to draw private carriages at Windsor, and thus became known as the Windsor Greys.

On the right as you go towards the exit are the **State Harness Room** and a display of saddlery. There are many historic items in these exhibits, including George IV's ornate saddle equipped with pouches for powder flasks, Queen Victoria's side saddle, and a beautiful set of hand-made pony harness presented to George V's children by the harness makers of England, and used today by the young princes.

There was a king's 'mewse' in the reign of Richard II. But in those days these were places where falcons were kept during their mewing or change of plumage. That royal 'mewse' was where Trafalgar Square is today.

Admission

The Royal Mews are open every Wednesday and Thursday, 2 p.m. to 4 p.m. except during Royal Ascot week, when the horses are at Windsor. Admission charge.

How to get there

Take the Underground to Victoria Station, which is only six minutes' walk away; or catch any bus going to Victoria.

8. THE TOWER OF LONDON

Though the Tower of London has a sinister reputation, it was once London's greatest diversion. It contained the royal menagerie, begun in 1235 when Henry III installed three leopards and a polar bear which was allowed (at the end of a long cord) to fish in the Thames.

Today, the Tower is mainly a museum. It was once a fortress, and an almost self-contained settlement, for behind the two protective walls were a palace, the mint, the arsenal, the Crown Jewels, the Royal Observatory and a state prison. It is still maintained as an arsenal with a garrison, and during both World Wars it was used as a prison for spies, traitors and state prisoners, including Rudolf Hess (Hitler's deputy) in 1941. The palace was completely destroyed by Cromwell. The mint and the observatory have been established elsewhere, but the Crown Jewels are still guarded and displayed at the Tower.

The Tower is a collection of Norman and medieval buildings dominated by the White Tower, built by William the Conqueror to protect (and to overawe) the citizens of London. The white stone was imported from Normandy.

All our sovereigns from William the Conqueror to James I used the Tower as a palace, always staying there the night before their coronation. The Tower was used as a state prison as early as 1100, but it was not until Tudor and Stuart times that the threat of being sent to the Tower hung over every political figure.

The Bell Tower

The outer wall of the Tower is surrounded by a deep moat. Entrance is through the Middle Tower and the Byward Tower, passing the **Bell Tower** on the left. Here **John Fisher, Bishop of Rochester,** and **Sir Thomas More,** who both refused to acknowledge Henry VIII as supreme head of the church, were confined. Poor Fisher, in his cold imprisonment, cried out for food, clothes and warmth. But he approached the execution block with dignity—and with the New Testament in his hand. Sir Thomas met his death with a quiet jest. He moved his beard carefully from the block, "for," he said, "though you have a warrant to cut off my head, you have none to cut my beard." The **Duke of Monmouth,** the illegitimate son of Charles II, who tried to capture the throne from James II, was also imprisoned in the Bell Tower.

Traitors' Gate

On the right is the Traitors' Gate through which many illustrious prisoners were taken to the Tower. One such prisoner was **Princess Elizabeth,** who was rigidly confined to the Tower for two months by her sister, Queen Mary, who feared Elizabeth's influence with the Protestants. As Elizabeth stepped ashore on to the steps of Traitors' Gate, she sank down and wept—the only time in her life that she showed fear.

The Bloody Tower

Turning left, we pass under the portcullis of the Bloody Tower, the only remaining original entrance to the wall defending the Inner Ward. It was built by Henry III. The portcullis is still in working order.

25

This is where the 'little princes', **Edward V** and **Richard of York,** were murdered in 1483. The bodies of the children were secretly buried. Their burial place was not discovered till nearly 200 years later, during Charles II's reign. A door was being cut through the wall of the White Tower, and the boys' bones were discovered. Charles had them reburied in Westminster Abbey.

Sir Walter Raleigh was also imprisoned in the Bloody Tower, by James I. This great seaman and explorer was confined to its close quarters for 13 years. "Only my father could keep such a bird in a cage!" cried young Henry, Prince of Wales. The prisoner's only exercise was pacing 'Raleigh's Walk', a few yards of wall that is still there. He never lost the affection of Londoners, nor of the sailors who passed up and down the Thames, and Raleigh would answer their greetings from his 'walk'. The main rooms have been restored and furnished as they would have been during his imprisonment.

Another popular prisoner here was **John Felton,** the young Army lieutenant who murdered the Duke of Buckingham (one of James I's favourites) in Portsmouth in 1628. The Duke was so unpopular that Felton had an almost triumphant entry to the Tower, and the townsfolk shouted encouragement to him all the way to his execution at Tyburn.

The Duke of Monmouth was possibly lodged in the Bloody Tower after the battle of Sedgemoor before being taken to the Bell Tower on the eve of his execution. The unscrupulous **Judge Jeffreys,** who treated Monmouth's men with such ferocity at the Bloody Assizes, was also imprisoned in this tower. (At the Assizes, he sentenced over 200 people to be hanged, and sent 800 into slavery in the Barbadoes.) When James II escaped to France after the landing of William of Orange, Jeffreys, disguised as a sailor, also tried to escape. But he was recognised in a tavern near Wapping by a man he had ill-treated. But he was not executed. He died of disease and drink.

Tower Green

Leaving the Bloody Tower and walking towards the White Tower, we come to Tower Green, where the famous ravens stalk about. The Green is in two parts. On the northern side is the site of the block, where a number of famous people were allowed the privilege of being executed in comparative privacy.

Among these were **Anne Boleyn,** the dark-haired second wife of Henry VIII (in 1536); the aged **Margaret, Countess of Salisbury** (1541); **Catherine Howard,** the fifth wife of Henry VIII, his 'rose without a thorn' (in 1542); **Lady Jane Grey,** uncrowned Queen of England for nine unhappy days (in 1554); and **Robert Devereux, Earl of Essex,** Queen Elizabeth's young favourite (in 1601).

The Countess of Salisbury had once been Queen Mary's governess. She was executed because of Tudor jealousy towards her family and her, the last of the Plantagenets. The poor old countess cried out that she was no traitor, and with her long white hair streaming behind her, she ran round and round the execution block till the headsman finally caught her.

All the Tower Green victims were executed with an axe except Anne Boleyn, who persuaded Henry to allow her to be executed with a sword. Anne went to the block with great courage. She jested that history would have no difficulty in finding a nickname for her. "They will call me", she declared, "la royne Anne sans tete!" But she grew so bright-eyed with terror that the executioner lost his nerve. He signalled his assistant to distract Anne's attention, snatched up his sword, and beheaded her unawares.

Beauchamp Tower

Between the two sections of Tower Green is a path leading to the Beauchamp Tower (dating from Edward I), the main prison for people of rank. This tower is famous for the inscriptions carved or scratched on the walls. One of the best is a carving by **John Dudley, Earl of Warwick,** of his family badge of a lion, a bear and ragged staff (1553). He added his name *John Dvdle* and surrounded the design with a garland of roses, oak leaves, gillyflowers and honeysuckle, to represent the names of his four brothers imprisoned with him. The rose was for Ambrose, the oak for Robert (later Queen Elizabeth's favourite, the Earl of Leicester)—from *robur,* an oak, gillyflowers stood for Guildford (husband of Lady Jane Grey), and the honeysuckle for Henry.

Twice scratched on the walls is also the word *Iane,* supposed to refer to Lady Jane Grey, probably carved by Guildford Dudley or one of his brothers. Guildford was executed on Tower Hill. From her window in the Yeoman Gaoler's quarters (now called the Queen's House), adjoining the Beauchamp Tower, Lady Jane saw her husband led out to his execution, and a little later saw his body brought back to be buried in the Chapel of St. Peter ad Vincula (St. Peter in chains) where she too was buried after her execution later that same day. In this chapel (standing to the north of the execution block) lie Bishop Fisher, Sir Thomas More, Anne Boleyn, Catherine Howard, Essex, Monmouth and many more illustrious prisoners.

The White Tower

In the centre of the eighteen acres of the Tower and its grounds stands the White Tower, its massive walls measuring from 11 ft. to 15 ft. thick.

This square-looking tower is not, in fact, square. Three of its corners are not right angles, and of the four turrets, three are

27

square and one (on the north-east) is round.

The Armouries, the national museum of arms and armour, are housed here, with exhibitions on every floor. This tower also contains St. John's Chapel, the oldest church in London.

The chapel is softly lit with rose-coloured lights. Here 'Bloody' Mary was married by proxy to Philip of Spain in 1554. The altar hangings were made from decorations used at Westminster Abbey for the coronation of George VI in 1937.

Arms and armour

There has always been armour in the Tower and the present collection is comprehensive and important. Particularly fine is the armour of Henry VIII, which, during his reign, was distributed between Greenwich (where there was a royal armoury), Westminster, Hampton Court and Windsor. **Henry VIII** enjoyed taking part in tournaments, and in the Armoury are tilt-armours of the period: generally heavier and less mobile than battle armour. In tournaments, the contestants passed left arm to left arm, with the lance aimed at the adversary's left side. So it was essential that the armour be strong and highly polished, so that the weapons—lance, sword or mace—would glance off and inflict the least damage.

As a young man, Henry was slim and athletic. Only a slim man could have worn the tonlet (skirted) armour made for him about 1510 (when he was 19). As he grew older, the king became fat, and he needed an immensely strong horse to carry him in his 1540 suit of armour (made in Greenwich). The skirt of this suit is ornamented with the brass initials H and K (Henry and Katherine of Aragon) with true lovers' knots. This is strange, as Henry was married to Catherine Howard in 1540.

Also from the royal armoury at Greenwich is the suit of armour made for Elizabeth's life-long friend and favourite, and her first Master of Horse, **Robert Dudley,** her 'Sweet Robin'. (They were imprisoned in the Tower at the same time. They had partly grown up together, and they met, and possibly fell in love for the first time, during imprisonment.)

In another case are suits of armour belonging to **Charles I** in about 1630, and to **Charles II** when he was the 12-year-old Prince of Wales, and facing these is a cabinet containing buff coats worn by Cromwellian soldiers. By tradition, one coat belonged to **Col. Francis Hacker,** who supervised the execution of Charles I in Whitehall on 30th January 1649.

By the time of the Restoration of Charles II, armour had become out-dated, and it was during his reign that the collection of armour and armoury was begun at both the Tower and at Windsor Castle. Over the years additions have been made, and continue to be made, but the old royal nucleus is still the main focal point, giving the Armoury a special link with the history of England.

Down in the dungeons (once the torture chamber) are the Mortar Room, showing bronze mortars, muskets, and the Cannon Room, with cannon, armour and pikes preserved in the Tower since the Civil War.

Escapes

There have always been armed men in the Tower, and prisoners were closely guarded. But there was naturally a certain amount of coming and going. Some of the prisoners were allowed visitors. (Raleigh's wife, for instance, took a house on Tower Hill, and visited him regularly during his long imprisonment, and his son Carew was born during this period.) Also, tradesmen had to supply the Tower with food and fuel, and it was these permitted visits that inspired the escape of **Lord William Seymour** and Lord Nithsdale.

Seymour, who was imprisoned for marrying Arabella Stuart, a cousin of James I, bribed a carrier delivering faggots and hay to give him a smock and a large hat, and allow him to take his place on the outward journey. He walked out of the Tower and escaped to France. In 1649, bearing no grudge against the son of the king who had imprisoned him, Seymour offered to take the place of Charles I on the scaffold.

Even more daring was the escape of **Lord Nithsdale,** one of three Scottish noblemen sent to the Tower after the failure of the Jacobite Rising of 1715. On the evening before the execution, his wife and women friends smuggled a hooded cape and skirt in to her husband's room. The visitors confused the guards by going back and forth, and in the confusion Lord Nithsdale, 'weeping' convincingly, was led out by one of his wife's companions. To give him time to make his way out through the gateway of the Bloody Tower and along the walk past the Bell Tower to the main entrance, Lady Nithsdale kept up the pretence of talking to her husband—and as she was leaving, turned back a servant who was carrying candles, with the plea that Lord Nithsdale was at his devotions and wished to be alone. Lord Nithsdale escaped to Italy disguised as a servant in the Venetian Ambassador's retinue. Lady Nithsdale joined him, and together they lived happily in Rome until Lord Nithsdale died—28 years after he had been sentenced to death in the Tower.

Yeomen Warders

Always on duty at the Tower are Yeomen Warders, who act as guides when available. The Yeomen Warders number 34 men from time-expired warrant and non-commissioned officers of the Army and the R.A.F. They are 'extraordinary members of the Queen's Bodyguard of the Yeomen of the Guard', but they form a quite separate body from the Yeomen of the Guard, which is probably the oldest royal bodyguard in the world, originating in the armed guards of the Saxon kings. These royal guards were newly appointed on the accession of a new soverign, and were known by various titles, including 'Cross Bowmen of the Household'.

Henry VII created the Yeomen of the Guard as a permanent body in 1485. During its long history, the scarlet Tudor dress and equipment has changed little, but its duties have become ceremonial and decorative. At one time the Yeomen guarded the king at home and abroad, even on the field of battle. Now their duties are confined to searching the vaults of Parliament House (with halberds and lamps in hand) on the day Parliament assembles (in case of another Guy Fawkes plot), and attending the sovereign at the opening of Parliament and on the day of the distribution of Maundy Money.

When Henry VIII was living in the Tower (as he did for some years) the Yeomen were in constant attendance on him. When he was away from the Tower, the fact that it was a royal residence was indicated by the twelve Yeomen who were permanently stationed there. They were the Tower Warders—and the distinction still holds good. Yeomen Warders take no part in the Court duties of the Yeomen of the Guard, whose scarlet costume is trimmed with black and gold and worn with a white ruff: their stockings are red, and their shoes are trimmed with red and white rosettes. They wear a cross-over belt (the chief difference between their costume and that of the Yeomen Warders of the Tower). Both Yeomen of the Guard and Yeomen Warders wear a Tudor garlanded hat.

The ravens

Ravens were once common in London streets, and were protected as useful scavengers. There have probably always been ravens at the Tower. They were said to fly in from the Essex marshes whenever there was an execution—and some of them stayed on. There is a legend that the Tower will collapse if the ravens leave, so some are always kept 'on the establishment'. They are cared for by a Yeoman Warden and are given a weekly allowance of 30p-worth of horseflesh.

Crown Jewels

Many people go to the Tower solely to see the Crown Jewels, and walk straight through the Bloody Tower entrance to the Jewel House and down the four flights of stairs to see these magnificent royal treasures.

But there is much splendour to see before going down.

On the ground floor is a display of many of Britain's most famous awards, including the Victoria Cross, George Cross,

Distinguished Service Order, Distinguished Service Cross, Military Cross, the Distinguished Flying Cross and the decorations and robes of various orders, like the Order of the Bath and the Order of the British Empire. Nearby are two golden coronation robes worn by every sovereign for the past 150 years, except Queen Victoria.

Also on the ground floor are a set of sixteen silver state trumpets and the Great Sword of State with its magnificent scabbard. This is carried before a sovereign as he enters Westminster Abbey for coronation, and at the State Opening of Parliament.

Most of the treasures of the Jewel House are connected with the coronation ceremony. After the execution of Charles I many of the royal ornaments were destroyed by Cromwell, even King Alfred's Saxon crown which had been used for the coronation of every English monarch up to then. Only three pieces escaped destruction: the Anointing Spoon, the Ampulla (a golden eagle holding the holy oil) and Queen Elizabeth's Salt (all three pieces are now displayed among the Crown Jewels).

A new set of crown jewels had to be made for the coronation of Charles II, and additional pieces have been added from time to time, usually following earlier designs.

Among the many crowns on show is a small diamond crown made for Queen Victoria, not much bigger than an apple, but one of the most important crowns is **St. Edward's Crown**— so called after Edward the Confessor. It was made for Charles II, probably from old crowns broken up during the Commonealth, but owing to its great weight (nearly 5 lb.) it is only used for the actual ceremony of coronation. It is then exchanged for the lighter **Crown of State,** which was made for the coronation of Queen Victoria and used at every coronation since then. This is also the crown worn by the sovereign for the opening of Parliament. Its oak-leaf patterned frame is set with more than 3,000 precious stones, mostly diamonds and pearls. Outstanding among these jewels is the **Black Prince's ruby,** a great irregular, uncut stone as big as a pullet's egg. This magnificent ruby was worn by Henry V at the battle of Agincourt in 1415. Also in this crown is the Stuart sapphire, taken to France by James II when he fled the country, and repurchased on the death of Cardinal Henry Benedict Stuart, the last of the House. In the upper cross is a sapphire which, according to tradition, was worn by William the Conqueror and recovered from his grave in the twelfth century.

31

Another beautiful crown is that made for the coronation of Queen Elizabeth the Queen Mother in 1937. It embodies the famous Indian diamond, the **Koh-i-noor** (or Mountain of Light). It is supposed to bring good luck to any woman who wears it, bad luck to any man.

It will help you to understand much of what you see if you visit the History Gallery, next to the Lanthorn Tower, where the story of the Tower, from 1078 to today, is set out and explained in words and pictures.

Admission

From March to October, 10 a.m. to 5 p.m.; rest of the year, 10 a.m. to 4 p.m.; Sundays (from March till late October), 2 p.m. to 5 p.m. (Not open on Sundays in winter).

The admission charge varies according to season. Special programmes can be organised for school visits, in some cases with free admission, and there are holiday activities. Enquiries to Education Centre, Waterloo Block, H.M. Tower of London, EC3 4AB. Tel: 01-709 0765, ext. 247.

How to get there

Much the easiest way is by District or Circle Line underground to Tower Hill station.

HMS BELFAST

Moored opposite the Tower, at Symon's Wharf, is HMS *Belfast* (11,500 tons), the largest cruiser ever built for the Royal Navy, and the last surviving big-gun ship of the Second World War. She is now a floating museum. Below decks are T.V. documentaries of her part in the sinking of the German battleship *Scharnhorst* in December 1943. HMS *Belfast* was the first of a fleet of 4,000 ships to arrive in Normandy for the D-Day invasion. She is a star attraction for boys of all ages.

Admission

Open daily except Christmas Day, 11 a.m. to 4.30 p.m. in winter, until 6 p.m. March to October. Admission charge (reductions for children and OAPs).

ALL HALLOWS BY-THE-TOWER

On the right, at the top of Tower Hill, is All Hallows by-the-Tower, the City's oldest church in that its foundation dates back to the time of the Saxon kings. Most of the church was destroyed in the last war, but the brick tower—the only example of Cromwellian architecture in London—survived, and was incorporated (with a beautiful, added spire) into the rebuilt church, rededicated in 1957.

All Hallows (meaning 'All Saints') is the guild church of the Toc H movement, founded during the First World War by Dr. P. B. ('Tubby') Clayton to carry the spirit of service into the years of peace. The Toc H lamp, a terracotta, boat-shaped lamp, burns in the church.

Toc H members from all over the world contributed to the rebuilding of All Hallows. New Zealand gave rimu panelling, the United States gave steel, Montreal gave a peal of eighteen bells, Canada as a whole presented tiles for the Nave. Maryborough, Queensland, where Dr. Clayton was born, donated a ceremonial chair. On the back are inscribed the words: *Fashioned with Zeal for your Reverend Rest. If you find me Strong and Thorough I was made in Maryborough.*

It was from the Cromwellian tower of All Hallows that Samuel Pepys and his wife watched the Great Fire of London sweep up the street in September, 1666. The fire reached the porch of All Hallows, and was only prevented from spreading further by the action of Admiral Sir William Penn, who ordered sailors to blow up houses in the fire's path.

This William Penn was the father of the **William Penn** (1644-1718) who founded Pennsylvania. He was born on Tower Hill and christened in All Hallows. On New Year's Day in 1662, Pepys invited William Penn and his sister to visit his home in Seething Lane (near the church), where they consumed a barrel of oysters.

The London Brass Rubbing Centre has a collection of replica brasses from all parts of the country assembled here for rubbing (see p. 59).

THE CEREMONY OF THE KEYS

Every night, at exactly seven minutes to ten, the Chief Yeoman Warder of the Tower begins his duty of locking up the Tower gates for the night.

The ceremony of the keys has been carried out every night through peace and war, for at least 700 years. The Chief Warder leaves the Byward Tower, wearing the traditional scarlet watchcoat and Tudor bonnet. In one hand he carries the candle-lit lantern; in the other a large ring bearing the Queen's Keys.

At the Wakefield Tower, the Chief Warder meets his escort of a sergeant and three men, one of whom is handed the lantern as the Warder takes his place with the soldiers.

After locking the outer gates, the party retraces its steps, locking each gate as it passes through. As the soldiers approach the Wakefield Tower, a sentry is standing by the Bloody Tower, awaiting them. He cries out:

"Halt! Who comes there?"

"The Keys", the Chief Warder replies.

33

"Whose Keys?"

"Queen Elizabeth's Keys!"

"Pass, Queen Elizabeth's Keys— and all's well."

Then, as the Keys approach the main guard, an officer (with drawn sword) gives the command: "Guard and Escort—present arms."

The Chief Warder steps forward and raising his Tudor bonnet, calls out: "God preserve Queen Elizabeth". To this, the guard and escort reply: "Amen", and the ceremony ends with the bugler sounding the Last Post as the Parade Ground clock strikes ten.

The ceremony—picturesque and rather spooky on a dark, misty night—may be watched by a small number of people every night. There are spotlights in the trees—and possibly ghosts looking on.

Write, enclosing a stamped addressed envelope, to The Deputy Governor (Administration), Constable's Office, H.M. Tower of London, EC3 4AB, giving a choice of several different dates. If you would prefer to ring and discuss available dates, the telephone number is 01-709 0765, ext. 213. There is no charge for admission.

9. THE LORD MAYOR'S PROCESSION

One of London's finest (and entirely free) days of celebration and pageantry is the first Saturday in November—the day of the Lord Mayor's Show.

It is the day when the newly elected Lord Mayor shows himself to the people of London on his way to the Law Courts, where he is formally presented to the judges of the Queen's Bench Division.

The procession goes from the Mansion House, past St. Paul's, along Fleet Street to the Law Courts, and then back again to the City along the Embankment. The floats taking part usually reflect the business interests of the new Lord Mayor, but the chief interest is the magnificent coach, built in 1757 and drawn by six perfectly matched brewers' horses. The coachman (who is so splendidly dressed in gold-laced scarlet livery that children sometimes think *he* is the Lord Mayor) wears a tricorn hat, and handles the six horses with reins of scarlet webbing. The coach itself, over 10 ft. high, is resplendent with gold, crystal and scarlet. The only brake on it is a wheel-brake operated by a footman walking behind.

The coach is escorted by pikemen of the Honourable Artillery Company of Pikemen and Musketeers. This military body was granted a charter by Henry VIII, and is thus the oldest regiment in the British Army, and probably in the world. From 1537 to the present day it has provided citizen soldiers for the defence of the country. H.A.C. men were amongst the troops inspected by Elizabeth at Tilbury in 1588. Milton, Wren and Samuel Pepys all served in this famous Company.

The H.A.C. pikemen in the procession are dressed in 1640 uniforms and their drill is based on a drill book of 1635. To equip themselves in their Cromwellian uniform takes half an hour. They have to don stockings, knee breeches, tunic, breast plate, back plate, and a pot helmet with a swirling feather. The weight of their armour and weapons is about 25 lb.

Royal visits

The Lord Mayor is an extremely important person in the City, but it is not true (as many people think) that the sovereign has to ask his permission to enter the City. The Lord Mayor does go to the City boundary (marked by the griffin in the middle of Fleet Street) when the sovereign is visiting the City, but this is to greet her. The sovereign halts just inside the City boundary, and there the Lord Mayor advances towards the royal coach, carrying the Pearl Sword of Elizabeth I, its point lowered in submission. He surrenders it with an expression of loyalty and it is returned to him with equal courtesy. The Lord Mayor then returns to his coach and precedes the sovereign through the streets of the City.

The Pearl Sword is said to have been presented to the City by Queen Elizabeth when she visited the Exchange in 1571, and bestowed on it the title of Royal Exchange.

When a sovereign dies, the Lord Mayor of London is one of the first people to be told. He immediately gets in touch with the Dean of St. Paul's and orders that the great bell shall be solemnly tolled.

---

10. THE CITY AND ITS STREET NAMES

When you are walking about exploring London (and really it is the only way to discover some of its secrets) take a note of the street names, for they will often tell you something of its development.

This is especially true in the City, the shape and area of which has always been much the same, ever since the building of the Roman wall, parts of which are still standing. (There is a sizeable section near Tower Hill underground station.)

The Old English word *straet* originally meant a paved street, and Henry I decreed that a street must be wide enough for 16 knights to ride abreast. Lanes were narrower, and had only to be wide enough for two men to roll a barrel of wine along them.

Many of the London streets that were important centuries ago are still important, such as Cheapside, Poultry, Threadneedle Street, Cornhill and Lombard Street—all of them near the Bank of England.

In a walk lasting an hour or so you can discover quite a lot about old London. Start at **Ludgate Circus.**

Ludgate was one of the old gates leading into the City. There was no King Lud, as some legends say. The name probably comes from the Old English *Ludgaet,* meaning back door or postern gate.

Many of the first London names were occupational names—reminders of the kind of life that once went on. Up Ludgate Hill, on the left, are **Ave Maria Lane, Amen Court** (set back a little), **Paternoster Steps** and **Paternoster Square.** Rosary makers and scripture text writers once lived here.

Walk round to the left of St. Paul's, past the statue of St. Paul himself among the plane trees, and you come into **Cheapside,** once the most important street in London. *Chepe* meant market. Cheapside was once considerably wider than it is today, and everything went on there—street trading, processions, bonfires, victory celebrations, executions, and the quick-flaring riots of the apprentices. (They particularly resented foreigners. The cry would go up "Prentices! Clubs!" and they would rush belligerently out of the shops.)

The first corner on the left off Cheapside is **Foster Lane,** from St. Vedast, or St. Vaast, a bishop of Arras who died about 540. (This is a good example of how names can change over the years.) Robert Herrick, the poet, was christened in St. Vedast church.

In Foster Lane is the Goldsmiths' Hall. The Goldsmiths' Company, incorporated in 1327, still assays and stamps gold and silver plate. Its hallmark is a leopard's head. Next on the left is Gutter Lane, then **Wood Street,** with an old plane tree preserved in the tiny churchyard-garden of St. Peter, Chepe, destroyed in the Great Fire of London. St. Peter's Keys, in gold, are incorporated into the railings round this small garden, to which there is no gateway. Next on the left is **Milk Street,** where cows once grazed and milk was sold. (Sir Thomas More was born there in 1478.) On the right is **Bread Street,** where bread was baked and sold. (John Milton was born there in 1608.)

Bow bells

Just past Bread Street is **St. Mary-le-Bow.** Every true Cockney has to be born within the sound of Bow bells which, according to legend, encouraged Dick Whittington to return to London as he was leaving disconsolately. The bells chimed out to him: "Turn again, turn again, thrice mayor of London". (In fact, he became Mayor three times—in 1396, 1397-8, 1406-7, and Lord Mayor in 1419-20.)

The curfew was rung by Bow bells for over 600 years, and a 9 o'clock bell signalled the end of the working day for the apprentices.

The name of the church comes from the bows or arches on which it was originally built. It was badly blitzed, and has been much restored. The first church had a small grandstand on the tower overlooking Cheapside, from which royalty could watch pageants and processions. There is a balcony on the tower Wren built. It holds the flagpole. Charles II once planned to watch a Lord Mayor's procession from there, but he was warned of an assassination plot and stayed away.

Beside the church is a statue of **Captain John Smith,** first governor of Virginia, whose life was saved (in 1608) by the thirteen-year-old Red Indian princess, Pocahontas. She later married Captain James Rolfe, and in 1616 became the first American to visit England. She died (of pneumonia) off Gravesend as she was returning to America. Mrs. Woodrow Wilson, wife of one of the United States' presidents (1913-1921) claimed descent from Pocahontas's son Thomas Rolfe.

Guildhall

Just past St. Mary-le-Bow is King Street, which runs right across Cheapside.

Go up King Street to the left, and there is **Guildhall,** or the Hall of the Corporation of the City of London. The Guildhall, open from 10 a.m. till 5 p.m. (on Saturdays, till 4 p.m.) is now used for municipal meetings, the election of the Lord Mayor and Sheriffs, and for State banquets. Some of the building was destroyed in the Second World War, but much of the Great Hall (originally built about 1411 to 1435) dates from its restoration in the seventeenth century.

As you enter Guildhall, just opposite the entrance is a door leading to the Ambulatory. On the left are large memorials to Lord Nelson (died 1805) and Sir Winston Churchill (died 1965). Set into the floor, and on the wall opposite Churchill, are brass tablets giving the standard measurements of inches, feet and the imperial yard.

At the far end of the hall is the Musicians' Gallery, guarded at each end by the famous figures of the legendary giants, Gog and

Magog. The ancestors of the present figures were made of wicker and were paraded in pageants, and their basket-work hands were used to present petitions. The present Gog and Magog are sombre creatures in green-brown war paint picked out in gold. They are over 9 ft. tall and weigh 15 cwt.

On the dais opposite the Musicians' Gallery is held the Court of Hustings, at which liverymen from all the craft-guilds gather to elect the Lord Mayor.

Famous trials

Less happy occasions connected with Guildhall are commemorated on a tablet. Anne Askew, a protestant martyr, was tried there in 1540. She was tortured at the Tower, carried in a chair to Smithfield, and there burnt to death.

The most important trial was that of the fifteen-year-old Lady Jane Grey, uncrowned queen of England for nine days, and her young husband, Lord Guildford Dudley. They were executed on the same day in 1554 (see page 27).

The twelve great companies

The banners hanging in Guildhall belong to the twelve great livery companies—the Mercers, Grocers, Drapers, Fishmongers, Goldsmiths, Skinners, Merchant Tailors, Haberdashers, Salters, Ironmongers, Vintners and Clothworkers. (There are over seventy other companies—each formed as a kind of friendly society to look after its members, and to fix wages and standards of workmanship.)

A Tudor adventurer

In front of Guildhall runs **Gresham Street,** called after Sir Thomas Gresham, founder of the first Royal Exchange in the reign of Elizabeth I.

Thomas Gresham was the son of a Lord Mayor of London, and was a leading member of the Merchant Adventurers. He came from a leading Norfolk family, and was an able and adventurous man, with an advanced understanding of economics, which in those days was known as 'political arithmetic'. He was sent to the Low Countries and Germany to negotiate loans for the Crown with wealthy merchants, and brought back 'gonne-powder and salt-peter', handled bullion, became a kind of secret agent for Elizabeth's Lord Burghley—and for Elizabeth's half-brother, Edward VI, he brought a 'great present of a payre of long Spanish silke stockings'.

At the height of his involvement with the Crown, Gresham crossed the Channel no fewer than 40 times in two years—no small adventure in itself in those days.

Proceed along Gresham Street to the left. On the right you pass **Old Jewry.** Until the expulsion of the Jews by Edward I in 1290, this was the main Jewish quarter in London—and the word itself incorporates an old form of plural, *ry*, also used in poultry and rookery.

'The Old Lady of Threadneedle Street'

Pass the end of Old Jewry, and turn right into **Princes Street.** In the distance you can see the top of the Monument to the Great Fire of London (see page 41). All along the left-hand side of Princes Street runs part of the **Bank of England,** which stands on an island site of more than three acres. On the outside, it is completely without windows—for security's sake—and only the entrance is open to the public.

'The Old Lady of Threadneedle Street' is the Bank's affectionate nickname, but look at the pediment. There sits 'the Old Lady' herself, her mantle billowing out in the wind. There is some doubt about the origin of the word 'threadneedle'. Perhaps three needles once appeared on a hanging sign of needle makers. Another theory is that threadneedle was a children's game, like oranges and lemons.

Seven great streets meet in the triangle dominated by the Bank of England; first Princes Street, then (clockwise), Threadneedle Street, **Cornhill** (where corn was once grown), **Lombard Street, King William Street, Queen Victoria Street,** and **Poultry.** (This is a continuation of Cheapside, and marks the area where poultry sellers once set up their stalls.)

Between Threadneedle Street and Cornhill is the **Royal Exchange.** This is a replacement of the one built by Sir Thomas Gresham, but on top is still his family crest—the famous golden grasshopper, 11 ft. long.

If you go 100 yards or so down Threadneedle Street and look up at the side of the Royal Exchange, you will see two figures (unnamed). On the right, in the long robes, is Dick Whittington. The other is Hugh Myddelton, who channelled drinking water to London from Hertfordshire—a great engineering feat—in the reign of James I.

Street of signs

Cornhill is a typical big commercial city street, but it is worth walking down **Lombard Street** to see the kind of hanging signs which were, before people could read, such a decorative and useful advertising feature of London life: the Black Horse of Lloyds Bank, the Golden Grasshopper of Martins Bank, a golden anchor and rope, a golden artichoke on a green ground, the charming Cat and Fiddle of the Royal Bank of Scotland, the Black Eagle of

Barclays Bank, and the three gold crowns of Coutts and Co. They all hang from wrought iron supports.

Lombard Street takes its name from the Lombards, who came to England from Lange Borde in the Lower Elbe district. When the Jews were expelled from England, the Lombards took over much of their trading and money-lending—and from the piles of unredeemed pledges which cluttered their storerooms comes the word 'lumber'.

The Mansion House and the Lord Mayor

Traffic near the Mansion House seems to come from all directions, so cross King William Street carefully, and there is the Mansion House, with its Corinthian portico and six pillars. The Mansion House is the Lord Mayor's official residence. It has ceremonial apartments, its own court of justice, and a prison. The public is not normally allowed into the Mansion House, though special public functions are sometimes organised.

The City is really a self-contained 'kingdom' with the Lord Mayor as its ruler. It has its own police force (recognisable by their red and white striped brassards), and inside the City limits the Lord Mayor takes precedence over everyone except the sovereign. The Lord Mayor has some interesting privileges. He is the first person to be told of the sovereign's death; he is the first person to be summoned to the Privy Council when a royal succession is proclaimed; he is hereditary Butler at the coronation; he is always told the day's password to the Tower of London; he is Admiral of the Port of London—and receives a warrant for a quarter of a buck in July and a quarter of a doe in November from the royal parks.

King John was the first king to grant London the honour of electing a mayor, but he wanted to inspect the City's choice, so he declared that each mayor should pay his respects to him at Westminster Palace. That was the origin of the present Lord Mayor's procession (see page 34).

The Temple of Mithras

Now walk a short way down **Queen Victoria Street,** and look at the remains of the Temple of Mithras, discovered during excavations in 1954. It was once underground and measured about 60 ft. by 20 ft.

The temple was built in Roman London, probably by the Roman garrison about the second or third century. The Mithraic religion was mainly a soldiers' religion. It demanded courage, faithfulness and endurance, but merchants also worshipped this god who seized and killed a sacred and terrible bull—the first living creature on the earth. The dying bull's blood nourished the earth, and living things began to flourish. A carved stone altarpiece from this temple, showing Mithras slaying the bull, is now in the London Museum.

Next is **Budge Row,** an underpass for pedestrians. Budge furriers once supplied lamb skin 'fur' or coney fur, used by wealthy citizens to decorate their clothes.

The catch about Cannon Street

Turn left at **Queen Street** (probably called after Charles II's queen, Catherine of Braganza), and you come to **Cannon Street.** This is one of the street names with a catch in it! It has nothing to do with cannon or cannonballs. It was originally one of the 'oc-cupational' streets and took its name from the wax chandlers and candlewick makers who worked there. Its Old English derivation was *candelwyrtha,* meaning a candlewright. John Stow, the Elizabethan chronicler, knew it as Candelweeke Street. By the time Samuel Pepys was writing in his diary some 60 years or so later, it had already become Canning Street—and from Canning to Cannon was an easy transition.

Turn back a short way up Cannon Street to look at the famous and somewhat mysterious **London Stone** set in the side of a building opposite the entrance to Cannon Street station. It is believed to have been used by the Romans as a central stone from which to measure road distances.

Next, turn back on your tracks, past the Mansion House un-derground station, and you are back again in Queen Victoria Street. Keep left, and after crossing Bread Street, turn right into **Friday Street,** now quite a short street but once the busy and smelly centre of the fish trade. (Fridays were celebrated as meatless days in memory of Good Friday.)

City of London Information Centre

Up Friday Street, and there is Cannon Street again. Turn left, and a short distance away is the circular Information Centre opposite St. Paul's. This centre is open on Mondays to Fridays from 9.30 a.m. till 5 p.m., and on Saturdays from 9.30 a.m. till 12.30 p.m. (01-606 3030). From here you can return to St. Paul's and to Ludgate Circus, where you began.

11. THE MONUMENT

Although The Monument is almost encircled by buildings, it is so tall it can be seen from many different City streets, and anyone with enough energy to climb 311 steps will be rewarded with a fine and wide view of the City and the river. At its top is an enclosed platform, and above that is a flaming gilt urn.

The Monument was built by Sir Christopher Wren to commemorate the Great Fire of London in 1666. It is a hollow fluted Doric column of Portland stone, 202 ft. in height—which is said to be the distance from its base to the site of the baker's shop in Pudding Lane where the Great Fire broke out on that dry, windy Sunday in September.

Admission

The Monument is in Fish Street Hill, near the northern end of London Bridge. There is an admission charge to go up the winding stairway. It is open on Mondays to Saturdays from 9 a.m. to 6 p.m. (April to September); from 9 a.m. to 4 p.m. (October to March), and on Sundays from 2 p.m. to 6 p.m. (May to September only).

How to get there

The easiest way is to take the underground to the Monument station—the Monument itself is only a few minutes' walk away up the hill.

Relic of Old London Bridge

Come out of the station into Fish Street Hill, and cross the road to look at one of London's small treasures—an elaborately carved sign (affixed to a rope-seller's shop). It was probably once an advertising sign on a rope-maker's or net-maker's shop on Old London Bridge. It shows two men in a double-ended peterboat (called after St. Peter). One is rowing; one is casting a net.

Fish Street Hill was once an important thoroughfare, leading directly to Old London Bridge. Now it leads nowhere. (The next London Bridge was built about 100 yards to the west.)

There were many good taverns in Fish Street Hill in the old days. In one of them in 1655 Samuel Pepys held his wedding feast after marrying his 15-year-old French wife.

The supporters of the shield in the City of London's armorial bearings were originally two lions, but in 1633 they were replaced by two dragons (possibly a reminder of the Welsh Tudor dragons). At the same time the motto was added: 'Domine dirige nos' (O Lord, guide us).

The arms are charged in the first quarter with a red dagger. This represents the sword of St. Paul, the City's patron saint, and NOT the weapon with which William Walworth, Mayor of London, slew Wat Tyler at Smithfield in 1381. The weapon

42

Walworth used, a basiliard, is still among the treasures of the Fishmongers' Company, of which he was a member.

Many of the lamp standards in London are decorated with the shield and its dagger. In other parts of London the lamp standards will often tell you what parish you are in. For instance, those in St. Martin-in-the-Fields are embossed with the figure of the saint leaning down from his horse to share his cloak with a beggar (plate 12).

12. ST PAUL'S CATHEDRAL

When Sir Christopher Wren demolished the burnt-out ruins of Old St. Paul's after the Great Fire of London with gunpowder and a battering ram, he found four layers of history on the cleared site.

The first church, founded in the early seventh century, was destroyed by fire. The second church, built of stone, was destroyed by the Vikings in the ninth century. The next church was burnt down in 1087. This was replaced by the Norman church, begun in the reign of William Rufus, which after the building of Wren's cathedral, has always been referred to as Old St. Paul's.

Old St. Paul's

Old St. Paul's, even larger than the present one, took nearly 200 years to build. During the fifteenth century trials for heresy and witchcraft were held in it, and those found guilty were burnt at the stake in Smithfield. But the building also witnessed ceremonies of great splendour, including the marriage of Arthur, Prince of Wales (Henry VIII's elder brother), to Katherine of Aragon in 1501.

In Elizabeth's reign the great spire, over 480 ft. tall, was struck by lightning and never restored. But the old church saw another great ceremony before it fell into final neglect and decay. Elizabeth attended a thanksgiving service there for the English victory over the Spanish Armada. With a fanfare of trumpets, she was driven right into the cathedral in a chariot drawn by four white horses.

In spite of some reconstruction, the church became a disreputable meeting place and gaming house. The nave was called 'Paul's Walk'. Men fought duels there, sold vegetables and coal, hired cut-throats and vagabonds, and led their horses through the building.

The ruin was completed during the Civil War, when Cromwell stabled his troopers' horses in the nave, and the men burnt the carved woodwork as firewood.

Wren's double dome

After the Great Fire, Christopher Wren (appointed Surveyor General and Architect by Charles II) was asked to design a new St. Paul's. His building was begun in 1675; the last stone was placed in position in 1710.

Throughout those 35 years Wren supervised the building of this great cathedral—and at the same time, the building of some fifty other City churches. Two or three times a week he was 'dragged up and down in a basket' to see how the work was progressing. By the time the famous dome was completed, Wren was an old man, too old to fix the last stone himself, and his son had the honour of placing it in position on the summit of the lantern.

When he was 86, Wren retired to his house at Hampton Court, but every year till his death in 1723 (when he was 91) he used to go and sit in silent contemplation of the **dome.** He is buried in the Crypt, where his epitaph, written by his son, reads: *Si monumentum requiris, circumspice.* 'If you would seek his monument, look around you'.

The dome *is* St. Paul's to many people. It is, in fact, a double dome. The outer one is of wood covered with lead. The elegant stone lantern on the very top, bearing a gilt ball six yards round and a cross 365 ft. above the ground, is not supported by the outer dome, but by an unseen brick cone rising from the inner dome. The ceiling of this inner dome, which is 218 ft. high, is decorated with scenes from the life of St. Paul.

Immediately beneath the great dome is a marble tablet marking the spot where the catafalque of Sir Winston Churchill stood during his state funeral in 1965.

The famous **Whispering Gallery** runs round the inside of the dome. What is whispered close to the wall on one side may be heard distinctly on the other side of the gallery.

Famous craftsmen

Part of Wren's genius lay in his ability to choose first-class artists and craftsmen to work with him. Chief among these were Grinling Gibbons, the woodworker who carved the organ case and wooden choir stalls, Charles Hopson, the joiner, who supervised the construction of the oak organ cases and the choir stalls, and Jean Tijou, responsible for the magnificent wrought iron sanctuary gates.

The **west front** of St. Paul's (facing Ludgate Hill) has a lower colonnade of twelve columns and an upper colonnade of eight columns. They are flanked by two bell towers. In the north-east tower is a peal of twelve bells. In the south-west tower is a clock face 17 ft. in diameter—and 'Great Paul', one of the largest bells in England. It is rung every day at 1p.m. It also tolls for two hours on the death of a sovereign, and for one hour on the death of the Archbishop of Canterbury, the Bishop of London, the Dean of St. Paul's, and the Lord Mayor.

'I shall rise again'

On the pediment of the great south door is a carving showing a **phoenix** rising from the flames. Beneath the phoenix is the word *Resurgam*. This recalls an incident that happened when measurements for the building were being made on the cleared site.

Wren asked a labourer to bring him a stone to mark the centre of his proposed dome. By chance, the man picked up part of an old, damaged tombstone. On it was the one word *Resurgam* ('I shall rise again'). Wren was so impressed by this incident that he commemorated it on his new church.

To appreciate the full beauty and glory of St. Paul's, stand first at the west end, just inside the main door, and look right down the nave to the marble High Altar and through the baldachino to the stained glass windows of the American War Memorial Chapel.

Then walk along the nave, past the huge Wellington memorial, to the great space beneath the dome.

Here you see the wonderful dome soaring above you, the spandrels decorated in mosaics, the lower arches showing the Crucifixion, the Entombment, the Resurrection and the Ascension.

A lion on guard

Much of the clutter of old memorials has been removed from the cathedral. The few still remaining are dominated by the pillared memorial to the Duke of Wellington (died 1852). This huge structure took 20 years to complete and is topped by the equestrian figure of Wellington himself.

In the South Transept (under the dome) is a memorial to Lord Nelson, showing Britannia pointing him out to two young boys, while the British lion lies on guard, snarling. Near the entrance to the Crypt is a memorial to Admiral Collingwood (died 1810), who took over from Nelson at the battle of Trafalgar.

The entrance to the **choir aisles** is on the north side, through fine iron gates by Jean Tijou. Beside the entrance stands a statue of Samuel Johnson (1784), the great lexicographer, in a Roman toga.

In this north aisle are the rear of the choir stalls, carved by Grinling Gibbons in the same meticulous way that he carved the front, and more beautiful Tijou gates, made from Sussex iron, splendid in black and gold with cherubs' heads, scrolls and acanthus leaves.

At the end of this aisle is the little **Chapel of Modern Martyrs,** which commemorates all known people who since 1850 have 'suffered death rather than renounce Christ'.

A step from this chapel leads to the **American War Memorial Chapel.** The floor has the words: *To the American Dead of the Second World War from the People of Britain.* A roll of honour in a glass and gold case records the names—hand-written on 473 pages of vellum—of 28,000 United States citizens serving with the Canadian, British and U.S. Armed Forces, who lost their lives between 1941 and 1945.

The walls of this chapel, formed by the outward curve of the apse, are lined up to the windows in English oak. Some of the panelling is delicately carved with festoons in limewood showing American flowers, fruit and birds, including a scrub jay, a scarlet tanager, an osprey, a quail, and a bobolink. Rising from the top of the panelling is an American eagle.

Passing through the American War Memorial Chapel and behind the High Altar (itself a memorial to members of the Commonwealth who died in the two World Wars) we come to the **Lady Chapel.** Here the Virgin and Child are framed in part of Wren's original organ screen.

A relic of the fire

In the south choir aisle is the memorial to John **Donne,** Dean of St. Paul's in Charles I's reign. It was scorched in the fire that burnt down Old St. Paul's. And inserted into the walls nearby are two fragments of the Temple of Herod.

In the south nave aisle is Holman Hunt's picture of Christ called *The Light of the World,* and at the west end of the nave is the oval **Chapel of St. Michael and St. George,** hung with banners of the Knights of the Grand Cross (G.C.M.G.).

Opposite this, in the north aisle, are **All Souls' Chapel** and the oval **Chapel of St. Dunstan,** used for daily celebration of Holy Communion and for private prayer. The All Souls' Chapel contains the Kitchener Memorial, with a recumbent white marble figure of the Field Marshal (lost at sea in 1916 when the cruiser *Hampshire* struck a German mine off the Orkney Islands when Kitchener was on his way to Russia). The two silver candlesticks at the side of this altar were made from trophies won by members of the Royal Rifle Brigade who were killed in the First World War.

The Crypt

The Crypt of St. Paul's has a quiet dignity, enhanced by the simplicity of the tombs and memorials.

Immediately below the dome is the tomb of Lord Nelson. He lies in a coffin made from the mainmast of the French ship *L'Orient,* enclosed in a sarcophagus of black and white marble. It was originally part of a tomb designed for Cardinal Wolsey, the original owner of Hampton Court. When Wolsey fell from favour, Henry VIII confiscated the tomb—and forgot about it. It was found at Windsor and used for Nelson's tomb.

Also in the Crypt is Wellington's tomb, a massive sarcophagus of Cornish porphyry standing on a granite base with lions' heads sunk into each corner. His huge black funeral chariot is also preserved here.

There are various bays in the Crypt devoted to sailors, soldiers, musicians and writers. Around Nelson lie famous seamen of another century, including Admiral Lord Jellicoe, Sir Roger Keys, Earl Beatty and Philip Vian.

One of the most interesting memorials in the Crypt is a link between the present St. Paul's and Old St. Paul's. This is a slab erected 'to Famous Dead buried in Old St. Paul's or whose memorials perished'. Among the names are poor Ethelred the Unready (1016), and Sir Philip Sidney (1586), hit by a musket shot at the battle of Zutphen. Thirsty with the pain of his shattered thigh, Sidney was offered a drink of water. He turned to another dying soldier, saying: 'Thy need is greater than mine!'

Admission

St. Paul's is open daily, 8 a.m. to 5 p.m. (7 p.m. in summer). Visitors may walk about at will, except on Sundays or when a service is in progress.

The Crypt is open every day (admission charge).

The Whispering Gallery (including the Ball when possible—it involves 727 steps to reach it!) is open 10.45 a.m. to 3.30 p.m. (admission charge).

---

13. MUSEUM OF LONDON

Standing high on London Wall in a corner of the Barbican raised walkway, near St. Paul's, is London's own new museum. Arranged on two floors surrounding a central glassed-in courtyard the displays tell the chronological story of London through the combined exhibits of the old London Museum and the Guildhall Museum as well as many acquired recently.

The light in the galleries is enticingly subdued, all the light being directed on to the exhibits. The story opens with the Old

Stone Age people of the Upper Thames 250,000 years ago, with Alan Sorell's pictures reconstructing convincingly how they might have looked and how they lived. Then look for the remarkable temple excavated at Heathrow and see what beautiful bronze weapons and armour were being made about the time Julius Caesar came.

When the victorious Romans built a bridge over the Thames London was founded. The Roman section of the museum is superb. From the house interior to the cutler's stall, most items are familiar: it would not be too difficult to live as a fairly well-off city-dwelling Roman. But look for the tiny seal boxes, secured to ensure that no one looked at the message, and at the legionary's armour which it must have been such a relief to remove!

After the Romans withdrew, the Saxons had little use for London and there is little to record until the decayed defences of the city were renewed as protection against the Danes (there is an impressive array of Danish battle axes and spearheads) and the city started to grow, slowly. By 1066 with its own militia it was strong enough for William the Conqueror to build castles around to control it, like the White Tower which you can see here.

From the medieval section onwards, the displays are as varied and rich as the city itself was becoming. The Cheapside hoard, buried by a jeweller, probably during an outbreak of the plague in 1603, shows exactly what he was offering for sale. Old London Bridge is beautifully recreated in John B. Thorp's diorama.

It would have been foolhardy to wear the lovely long pointed slippers to walk the filthy streets—look for the wooden pattens worn to raise the feet above the mud. Before you experience the Fire of London at the end of this floor look out for Charles I's boots (very neat) and the tennis ball made of leather and stuffed with dog's hair. (There is a fire engine, too, after the Fire!)

Appropriately everything seems bigger downstairs in rebuilt London, as you move from the eighteenth through to the twentieth century, through rooms and offices and past shops. There are examples of every kind of fine workmanship: wealthy Londoners could afford the best. The cell from Newgate Prison is a sombre reminder of those who failed. Look for the late Stuart surgical instruments. One hopes the surgeon knew more about the body than the little white figure suggests!

Our century starts with the suffragettes—the only place where you will find a Liberal cat with a woman in its mouth—quickly followed by a dark war scene with a Zeppelin in the sky. The gaiety of the thirties gives way to the last war—look for the story of the fire bomb—and the final magnificent exhibit—the Lord Mayor's coach. It stands, surrounded by water to keep the wood moist, awaiting the raising of the drawbridge ahead when it is taken out for the Lord Mayor's Show in November.

1. *Elephants at the London Zoo.*

2. The drawbridges of Tower Bridge weigh 1,000 tons each and can be raised in a minute and a half.

3. William the Conqueror was crowned at Westminster Abbey and all British sovereigns since—except Edward V and Edward VIII—have been crowned here.

4. A reconstructed scene at the London Dungeon shows what it was like inside the home of a poor family afflicted by the plague.

5. This is Tipu's Tiger at the Victoria and Albert Museum. The tiger contains a mechanical organ which gives out the cry of a man being attacked.

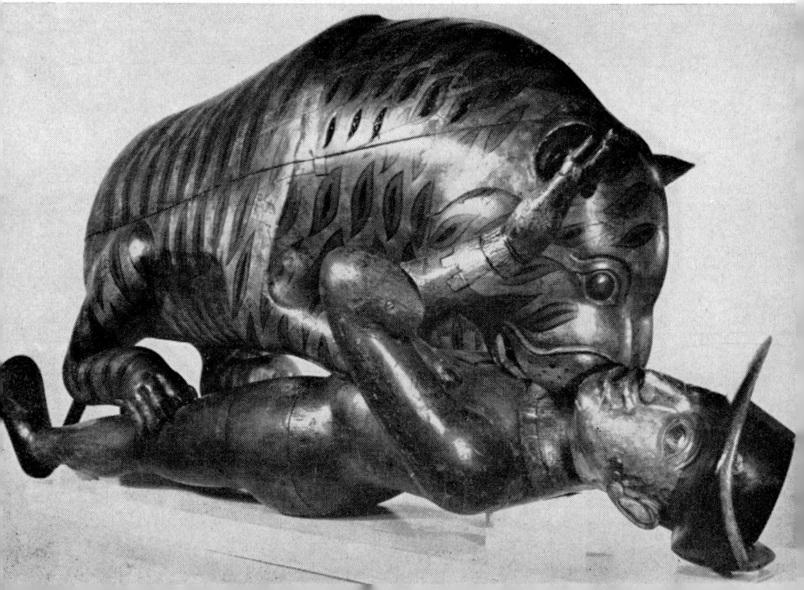

6. *The longest rowing race in the world is from London Bridge to Chelsea for Doggett's Coat and Badge. Thames watermen compete annually.*

7. *The blade of the guillotine which executed so many victims of the French Revolution is in the Chamber of Horrors at Madame Tussaud's.*

8. The wax effigy of Charles II is in the exhibition at Westminster Abbey. The face was modelled at his death and is considered a close likeness.

9. Royal Salutes are fired in Hyde Park on several occasions during the year. They are fired by the Royal Horse Artillery on 13-pounder guns.

10. Fountains at Kensington Gardens where Queen Victoria spent much of her childhood.

11. *The statue of Peter Pan in Kensington Gardens is surrounded by fairies and animals.*

12. *Lamp - posts near St. Martin's - in - the - Fields depict St. Martin giving his cloak to a beggar.*

Admission

Open weekdays except Monday, 10 a.m. to 6 p.m. and on Sundays 2.30 p.m. to 6 p.m. Closed Christmas Eve, Christmas Day, Boxing Day, New Year's Day and Good Friday. There are special facilities for school parties, which must be booked in advance through the Education Officer. Those who cannot climb the steps to the high walk should telephone for special directions. Three wheelchairs and nine pushchairs may be borrowed. The Museum number is 01-600 3699.

How to get there

Three underground stations, Barbican, Moorgate and St. Pauls are close by, as are buses 8, 22, 25, 43 and 11.

THE LONDON DUNGEON

Devised specially for those who want to know what it really was like, here is an exhibition of the gruesome and gory side of British history from the Dark Ages until the end of the seventeenth century, housed in dark chilly vaults under London Bridge station. Historically accurate, it tells a cruel yet illuminating story.

As you enter you are immediately aware of the strange atmosphere, emphasised by the musty smell, the strange sounds and the flickering candlelit interior ahead. Sawdust muffles your footsteps as you tear yourself from one scene to gaze at another. The Druids, dark priests of the iron age, perform a sacrifice. Boadicea kills a Roman soldier. A priest desperately grasps the altar cloth to cover Thomas a Becket, murdered at prayer.

The most pitiful scene is the plague-ravaged home of a poor family: the squalor and harsh cruelty of disease is conveyed as clearly as the more obvious horrors of the tortures of the Tower further on.

Admission

Open daily 10 a.m. to 6 p.m. (April to September), 10 a.m. to 4.30 p.m. (October to March). Admission charge. Group tickets available.

How to get there

The London Dungeon is at 28/34 Tooley Street, S.E.1. London Bridge main line and Underground stations are two minutes walk away. Buses which pass nearby are 35, 44, 48, 70, 133, 501, and 513 (Monday to Friday).

At the other end of Tooley Street (near Tower Bridge) is Skate City, the first London skateboard centre, where you can take a skateboard and hire protective clothing, if necessary, and whizz around the concrete, sandbagged circuit.

14. THE WALLACE COLLECTION

The Wallace Collection was gathered together largely by the fourth Marquis of Hertford, who spent most of his life in Paris. It was extended and eventually brought to London by his natural son Richard (who used his mother's name) and his French wife. They established a fine home in Hertford House, once the Spanish Embassy.

After Richard's death, his widow bequeathed the collection to the nation on condition that the Government provide a house for it in central London, and display it 'unmixed with other objects of art'. The Government therefore purchased Hertford House, where the treasures are beautifully displayed.

That, very briefly, explains how pictures, china, sculpture, furniture, glass, tapestry, arms and armour, clocks, snuff-boxes, chandeliers and jewellery collected by a Marquis of Hertford whose name was Seymour-Conway have come to be known as the Wallace Collection.

The Marquis began his collection by specialising in French art of the eighteenth century, and apart from the exceptional displays of arms and armour, the great treasures of the Wallace Collection are the paintings, furniture and ornaments of the Louis XV period.

Arms and armour

The range of European armour here is unrivalled in England outside the Tower of London. One magnificent set of equestrian armour is a fifteenth-century Gothic war harness made in southern Germany. The horse's shell-like fluted armour (edged inside with fur) hangs from a chain mail which protects its neck and mane. This armour is a great rarity and represents German Gothic armour at its best.

The collection of firearms is also outstanding—mostly sixteenth and sevententh-century German wheel-lock guns, rifles and pistols, often carved or inlaid with staghorn, mother-of-pearl or silver. There are also powder flasks, pistols made for Louis XIV of France, daggers, crossbows, a sword and a right-handed gauntlet belonging to Henry, Prince of Wales (elder brother of Charles I), and a hunting sword given to the fourth Marquis of Hertford (the man who began it all) by Napoleon III.

Part of the great charm of the Wallace Collection is that it is on display in one of the great houses of the period, though it contains a marble staircase grander than most. Its balustrade of forged iron and gilt bronze was made for Louis XV. It is a wonderful example of craftsmanship, decorated with the French royal monogram of interlaced Ls and with the sunflower emblem of French kings. It was scrap-iron when Sir Richard Wallace acquired it.

Admission

The Wallace Collection is open on weekdays from 10 a.m. to 5 p.m. and on Sundays from 2 p.m. to 5 p.m. Closed Christmas Eve, Christmas Day, Boxing Day, New Year's Day and Good Friday. Telephone: 01-935 0687.

How to get there

Hertford House, where the Wallace Collection is, is in Manchester Square, off Oxford Street, more or less at the back of Selfridges.

BRASS RUBBING

If you have ever taken a copy of the design on a coin by putting paper over it and scribbling hard with a pencil until the picture comes up you have the basic idea of brass rubbing. English churches have a variety of memorial figures of all sorts of people from knights in armour to small children: reproductions of these have been made in metal and are now collected together in brass rubbing centres so that you can choose your subject and do the rubbing without travelling to the church. There is a fee for each rubbing you take, depending upon the size of the brass, and the fee includes all the materials, the paper and wax (called heelball) that you use. There is expert guidance and helpful advice available so that the complete beginner can achieve a very satisfactory result first go, and come away with an attractive wall decoration that is all his own work. The brass rubbing centres get very busy during the summer and it is best to arrive early to get the widest choice of brasses to rub.

At present there are collections at St James's Church, Piccadilly, 10 a.m. to 6 p.m. (12 p.m. to 6 p.m. Sunday), at All Hallows Church beside the Tower of London, 10.30 a.m. to 6 p.m. (12.30 p.m. to 6 p.m. Sunday), Westminster Abbey and St Margaret's Church, Westminster, 9 a.m. to 5.30 p.m. (closed on Sunday).

---

15. BETHNAL GREEN MUSEUM AND THE GEFFRYE MUSEUM

The Bethnal Green Museum is a perfect museum for children. The toy collection, which is such a feature of it, is now one of the most important in the country. Toys as we know them have only been given to children for about 100 years. Before that, children were kept busy at 'leisure tasks'. Some of the first toys were designed to be educational, such as the 1850 jigsaw showing the working of a dockyard and others, more familiar, which made up into maps of England. See, too, the colourful charts of the kings and queens of England with brief, biased descriptions of each monarch underneath! The fascinating collection of toy soldiers shows how long fathers and sons have enjoyed playing wargames. The American Army Band is a delightful modern example and at the end of the cabinet is a group of figures so tiny that they have to be viewed through a magnifying glass.

The big centre space of the building is usually taken up with a temporary exhibition relating to children. On the left is the small reading area where you will find all sorts of books for all ages, some for a quiet browse, others relating to the museum.

Down in the basement there are curious mechanical devices with which the Victorians produced moving, flickering pictures—their names usually end in 'scope'—and some beautiful puppets and theatrical toys. The art room is there too, open to young visitors on Saturdays.

Dolls' houses

The Bethnal Green Museum has a fine collection of dolls' houses. The earliest is the Nuremberg Dolls' House, made in 1673. It has a stocking stretcher on one wall, and a baby walker to keep the baby safe while the mother says her prayers by the four-poster bed.

One of the semi-educational toys is the Nuremberg kitchen, made in 1700. It is just a three-sided box containing everything a little girl of that period would need to know; model kitchens such as this were used for instruction in German schools. Under the dresser is a hen-coop where hens were kept till they were needed for dinner. There is also a turning spit in front of the oven, and balancing scales hanging against the wall.

There is also a most realistic 1840 model of a butcher's shop, displaying all the cuts of meat and whole carcases, and the butcher himself standing at the door.

The dolls

The remarkable collection of dolls is arranged to show how dolls have developed since 1750. Perhaps the early stiff wooden dolls are not very cuddly but they are beautifully dressed.

Small girls find 'Princess Daisy' the star attraction. She is an English doll (with an elaborate Dutch layette), and was given to Queen Mary in 1899 for her own baby, Princess Mary. She has a pink satin and cream lace cradle, and her own pearl necklace with a real diamond clasp.

Local collections

Bethnal Green Museum is housed in an interesting Victorian building with iron roofs and its collection of local products includes silk from Huguenot weavers who settled in the district.

Admission

Open weekdays (including Bank Holidays) except Friday 10 a.m. to 6 p.m., Sundays 2.30 p.m. to 6 p.m. Closed Christmas Eve, Christmas Day, Boxing Day and New Year's Day. For information about activities for children in groups or as individuals in term and during holidays telephone 01-980 2415.

How to get there

The Bethnal Green Museum is in Cambridge Heath Road, E.2. It is only five minutes' walk from Bethnal Green underground station (on the Central Line).

Geffrye Museum

The Geffrye Museum is housed in the former almshouses of the Ironmongers' Company. Most of the collection of lovely furniture and woodwork from 1600 to 1939 is effectively displayed in a series of period room settings created by Marjorie Quennell when she was Curator in 1935.

From the entrance hall runs the Georgian Street, starting with a fully equipped woodworker's shop. Off the long corridor open the room settings (with a library halfway down and a coffee shop behind) and beside each room are detailed descriptions of particular items. It is interesting to see the way living gradually became easier. The open hearth kitchen is fascinating—the large iron implements and utensils are beautifully devised—look for the 'idleback' to help tip a very hot kettle and the toasting forks.

The highly carved Elizabethan chairs and chests and the simple elegant eighteenth-century furniture are lovely to look at but nineteenth-century furniture looks more inviting to sit on! The Victorians obviously loved lots of ornaments, like the dried flowers under glass. In the Voysey room there is a cylinder phonograph and an early telephone. Although the plain, uncarved furniture in the 1930s rooms looks old-fashioned yet familiar, items like the wireless and television sets seem very quaint!

Pre-booked school visits are part of the day-to-day life of the museum, and Saturday and holiday activities are very varied. On Saturday worksheets and puzzles linked to the exhibition are available. It is essential to book group visits. Telephone 01-759 8368.

Admission

The museum is open on weekdays except Mondays 10 a.m. to 5

p.m. and on Sundays 2 p.m. to 5 p.m. It is closed on Christmas Day and Boxing Day.

How to get there

The Geffrye Museum is in Kingsland Road, Shoreditch, E.2., ten minutes walk from Liverpool Street (left) or Old Street (right then left at junction) Underground stations. Buses 22, 22A, 48, 67, 97, 149 and 243 stop at the museum.

London's canals, which declined as industry switched to rail and road for transport, have been reviving in recent years as recreation areas. There are many pleasant walks along the towpaths (described in 'Discovering London's Canals' in this series) and there are trips along some stretches during the summer. At Little Venice (nearest Underground, Warwick Avenue), the junction of the Paddington and Regent's Canals, British Waterways Board waterbuses ply around Browning's island in the centre (named after the poet) and down Regent's Canal past the Zoo. Trip boats operate from here, Port a Bella at Ladbroke Grove (Paddington Canal) and from Camden Locks at Camden Town (Regent's Canal), and there are restaurant boats, too.

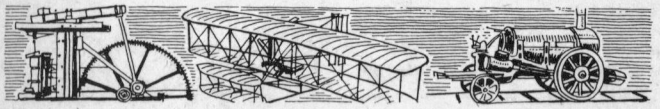

---

16. SCIENCE MUSEUM

Children visiting the Science Museum should make a bee-line for the **Children's Gallery,** in the *rear* part of the basement. There are two entrances: one near the locomotives and old cars, the other by the fire engines.

As well as dioramas showing the development of transport, from a man carrying game on his back perhaps 10,000 years ago, and pack horses and a single-masted ship of 1400 to a modern motorway, there are countless push-button working models of various delights from waterwheels to a teleprinter.

A clock that tells hours, days and months

Many of the models and exhibits actually work, including engines of all kinds and a periscope from H.M.S. *Tiptoe* (1945) that gives a view of both the ground floor and the first floor. It emerges near a diesel-electric locomotive and (on the wall) a blue and gold clock, an exact (though smaller) replica of the famous astronomical clock at Hampton Court. It tells the hour, the day of the month, the month itself, the number of days since the beginning of the year, and the phases of the moon.

Exploration gallery

Leave yourself plenty of energy to enjoy the dark, exciting Exploration gallery where you can see a life-size model of the Apollo moon-base with the first two men on the moon, Armstrong and Aldrin, and the actual Apollo 10 spacecraft and other items. A replica of a submersible is the centrepiece of Underwater Exploration, an equally challenging area to the explorer. As you wander through the gallery you can see yourself and your family on television or in the form of 'heat pictures' where differences in temperatures appear as different colours. There are four other exploration topics.

The Rocket and Puffing Billy

Out in the Centre Hall you find the Transport exhibits, one of the most famous of which is George Stephenson's *Rocket* locomotive constructed in 1829—and in the possession of the museum since 1863. The *Rocket* was built to compete for a premium of £500 for a loco capable of hauling a specified load at 10 m.p.h. Only the *Rocket* completed the course, running 35 miles at an average speed of 14 m.p.h.

Puffing Billy, the oldest locomotive in the world, constructed in 1813, is here, and nearby is the Great Western *Caerphilly Castle*, a 1923 loco, which travelled nearly two million miles before being withdrawn from service in 1960. A platform has been built alongside, so that visitors may look into the cab.

Amongst this splendour of the past is a York to London Royal Mail coach of 1827 (up to 1784 the mail had been carried on horseback by postboys) — and a more leisurely vehicle, a lovely green gypsy caravan with big yellow wheels, red decorations, and its own letter box in the small back door. And there are old motor-cars and trams.

On the first floor of the museum is a homely scene of a Jersey cow being milked—but the secret of its fascination lies in seeing the milk gush up (time after time) into a glass container. Nearby are a series of busy dioramas showing farmers and agricultural machinery at work at different seasons of the year—digging post holes, sawing wood, harvesting beet and digging potatoes.

Near the escalator is an impressive automated diorama showing a team on a cold dark North Sea rig, drilling for gas, part of the story of gas from the ancient Chinese to the present day.

The first powered flight

An escalator leads up to the **Aeronautics Gallery** on the top floor, where two of the star attractions are a Battle of Britain

Spitfire — P9444 — and a Hurricane — L1592. Almost as popular is a replica of the Wright Flyer, in which two American brothers, Orville and Wilbur Wright, made the first successful flight (in 1903) in a powered aeroplane. The flight lasted only 12 seconds.

One of the reasons the Wright brothers turned to powered flight was the death after a crash of a much-respected glider designer and pilot, Otto Lilienthal. He produced a series of gliders between 1891 and 1896, and made over 2,000 short flights. One of his gliders is strung from the ceiling in this gallery, showing how his body was strapped between the wings, leaving his arms free. This glider has bamboo longitudinal members, willow wing ribs hinged to the centre section of the frame, and fabric wings shaped like a bird's.

Among the other exhibits is the nose portion of a Gloster Meteor F3 (the plane from which the first ejection of a man in a parachute took place in July 1946), the Cody biplane of 1912, a rocket engine, and many models, including one of the Anglo-French supersonic transport Concorde, which made its maiden flight in March 1970. In the same display case is a model of a Voisin biplane, which made the first cross-country flight in Britain, in 1908 — at 34 m.p.h.

Prisoner-of-war models

On the half floor below the planes are model sailing ships of all kinds, including luggers, oyster smacks, a seven-masted schooner, dhows, and a lightship. Near them are model steam ships, including the *Great Eastern,* the largest vessel afloat from 1858 to 1899. There is a model of the 83,673-ton *Queen Elizabeth,* an 1824 figurehead from H.M.S. *North Sea,* and a case full of models made by French prisoners of war between 1793 and 1815, when they were interned at Dartmoor, Portchester Castle and Norman Cross. These little ships were made of wood or bone, chiefly ivory, and are highly prized though not strictly accurate. The pride of the collection is *The Prince* (1670)—possibly the finest ship model of its period in existence. This was once the flagship of the Duke of York (later James II). It was designed by the great Phineas Pett, who had operated as a privateer off the Barbary Coast.

A highly popular section on the top floor is the BBC Ceefax T.V. screen. A store of information can be tapped and flashed on to the screen by pressing a button — provided you know what page you require. Almost certainly you will have to wait for your turn.

You will find an entertaining use for computers in a booth where, for a fee, your photograph is taken (and shown upon a screen) and in no time at all a computer has printed it on to paper. It can then be transferred to a T shirt.

Admission

Open on weekdays 10 a.m. to 6 p.m., and on Sundays 2.30 p.m. to 6 p.m. Closed on Christmas Eve, Christmas Day, Boxing Day, New Year's Day and Good Friday.

School parties are welcome, but teachers or parents acting as escorts are advised to make a preliminary visit, or to write in, to make sure that a gallery or exhibit of particular interest is available for inspection.

Special demonstration-lectures can be arranged to suit the needs and interests of any group of children from 10-year-olds upwards. Parties of handicapped children can be given special assistance, but the museum appreciates notices in writing well in advance.

Requests for demonstration-lectures, lecture tours and tickets for special lectures should be sent to The Director (Lecture Service), The Science Museum, South Kensington, London, SW7 2DD (telephone 01-589 6371).

Children may eat packed lunches in the Children's Lunch Room on the first landing.

How to get there

The museum is only a few minutes' walk from South Kensington Underground station, and buses passing near include Nos. 14, 30, 74 and 97.

The quit-rent ceremony held in London every October dates back at least 700 years. The quit-rents are handed over at the Law Courts to the Queen's Remembrancer by the City Solicitor for two properties, 'The Forge', near St. Clement Danes, and 'The Moores', in Salop. Six shoes from Flemish war horses, 61 nails, and a hatchet and billhook are the rents paid. At the end of the ceremony they are returned to the City for use the following year. For the few seats available apply to the Queen's Remembrancer, Room 120, Royal Courts of Justice, London WC2A 2LL.

---

17. NATURAL HISTORY MUSEUM

The public galleries of the Natural History Museum are undergoing major changes: according to when you go some familiar exhibits may not be on view or may have been moved. If you plan to visit a particular gallery or specimen it would be wise to telephone the Museum to check.

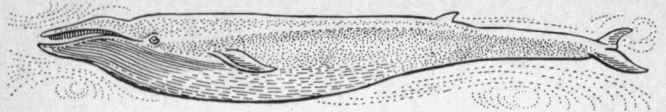

Hall of Human Biology

It is all part of a plan to increase the pleasure of people of all ages in learning about natural history. The new Hall of Human Biology makes a splendid beginning. You reach it from the Bird Gallery on the ground floor and enter Section A, the first of ten sections in a very large exhibition (which is really too much to take in on one visit).

Each section has a theme, such as growing, and is illustrated by diagrams, models, slide shows, cartoons, games to play, mechanisms to manipulate. Huge cross sections of cells and organs display their amazing complexity. You move your own muscles to manipulate devices showing how muscles work. Your reactions to emergency situations show how the hormones carry messages for your protection. You can discover that you have three types of memory, how to distinguish between them and how you learn. After an energetic tour you will have discovered quite a lot about yourself.

By 1980 the Dinosaurs will be in the entrance hall with 84 ft. Diplodocus and gigantic Tyrannosaurus welcoming visitors in place of the elephants and rhinos then on show elsewhere. In one of the side galleries here, look for the fish which surprised everyone when one was caught in the waters off Madagascar in 1938. The coelacanth was thought to have been extinct for seventy million years! Rivalling this display in interest is the new **Fossil Mammal Gallery.** Here is the skull of Baluchitherium, the largest land mammal that every lived, and a complete skeleton of Arsinoitherium, which was almost as large.

The **Whale Room,** in the north corner of the ground floor, has a life-sized cast of a 90 ft. blue whale—made to measurements taken from a series of whales caught in Antarctic waters. Blue whales are the largest of all known animals, living or extinct.

Suspended from the ceiling are actual skeletons of five species of commercially important whales—so commercially important that they have been hunted almost to the point of extinction.

The dead dodo

Birds are shown in a long gallery immediately to the left of the main entrance. The favourite is undoubtedly the dodo, from Mauritius—extinct and 'as dead as the dodo' since 1693. Amongst the other exhibits is a case showing different kinds of birds' nests. Two of the most interesting are the Indian tailor bird's, which neatly stitches two long leaves together to hold the nest, and the golden oriole's, with a neat nest built between two twigs.

British birds are grouped together in their own pavilion, with a domed roof representing the sky. Across this goes a flight of mallard, in formation, and on a lonely pinnacle of rock sits a golden eagle.

Dioramas of Africa

When the new ecology exhibition opens in the western gallery it will illustrate how natural things interrelate, drawing most examples from an English oak woodland and from a rocky shore, with lots of specimens, models, interactive machines and dioramas. Leading from this gallery is the Rowland Ward Pavilion, where three spectacular dioramas have been arranged. (There are seats here, very welcome, as these exhibits are full of interest and worth looking at for a long time.)

One diorama shows a water hole in North Kenya, with two adult giraffes standing by the water with a four-day-old giraffe at their feet. Gazing at them is a kudu, with a red-billed oxpecker on its back. On the ground are a gaggle of Egyptian geese and a family of baboons. The second diorama is a darkly green corner of the Ituri forest in Africa. Among fungi and vines are two okapis. The third diorama shows sable antelopes using the sun-baked top of a termite colony as a look-out in a parched Angola landscape.

At the end of the balcony is a much-needed cafeteria.

The Children's Centre and Natural History Club

There is a Children's Centre in the North Hall, open on Saturdays 2 to 4 p.m. and during school holidays 10.30 a.m. to 12.30 p.m., 2 to 4 p.m. (not Sundays). Children between the ages of 10 and 14 who are really interested in natural history can join the museum's Natural History Club (after submitting an entrance project). The Club meets every Saturday morning except during August. Apart from working on their own projects, members may attend films and talks, and once a month go on a field trip with Children's Centre staff, exploring pond life, collecting fossils, insects and plants, or visiting other museums. Though children have to pay their own expenses on these trips, there is no entrance fee or subscription, and drawing paper and chalks are supplied. There is a similar club for younger children. Ask at the Children's Centre. For educational information ring 01-589 6323.

Admission

Open Mondays to Saturdays 10 a.m. to 6 p.m., Sundays 2.30 p.m. to 6 p.m. The museum is closed on Christmas Eve, Christmas Day, Boxing Day, Good Friday, and New Year's Day.

How to get there
    The nearest underground station is South Kensington. Buses to take are 14, 30, 45, 74 and 207.

Trafalgar Square at dusk is filled with spiralling and wheeling flocks of starlings which are a feature of 'London by night'.

Starlings feeding in the suburbs gather in small groups towards sundown, and the small groups join up with larger and larger groups until, in flocks of thousands strong, they fly off to their habitual roosts in London. The birds fly along set 'flight lines' and settle in dense concentrations around Trafalgar Square and St Paul's Cathedral.

In June and July, the peak period for the starling invasion (when young birds are joining in), the main roost is Duck Island in St. James's Park. Over 90,000 have been counted on this small island alone.

The nightly invasion of London by the starlings still puzzles experts. It is only about 50 years since they first began coming and it is a remarkable change of habit in birds that normally go to communal roosts in the country.

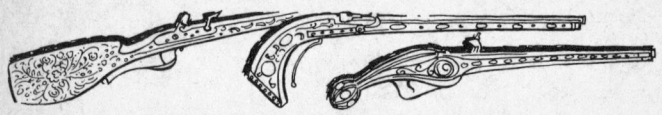

---

18. VICTORIA AND ALBERT MUSEUM

    This museum specialises in fine and applied art of all countries, styles and periods. There is so much to see that it is best to select particular exhibits that interest you. For example, most people want to see the Costume Court and Tipu's Tiger (plate 5).

    From the main entrance go through the shop and turn left, walking through Oriental galleries — see if you can find the beautiful Javanese shadow puppet and a Tibetan cousin to a guitar — until you come to Costume Court on the right and Tipu's Tiger ahead.

Tipu's Tiger

    Tipu's is a wooden tiger. He is mauling a startled-looking man who has managed to keep his hat on. The animal contains a miniature mechanised organ which, when operated by a push-button, gives out the cry of the mauled man. It is not very convincing, but a bit scary to the very young. The tiger was probably made in Mysore about 1795. It is not always shown in the same place, so if you particularly want to see this ask one of the attendants.

Costume Court

This museum has some of the finest period clothes in the world. Look especially for the doublet and hose said to have been worn by James I before he became king in 1603—the plum-coloured velvet is topped off by a large stiff white collar which stands out like a huge pie frill! See how fine and ornate some of the Court dresses were and how difficult to wear. There are period dolls, too, with sets of tiny corsets, slippers and mittens, for every occasion.

The 'giraffe piano'

Upstairs from Costume Court is the Musical Instruments Gallery. Probably the most curious exhibit is the 'giraffe piano', equipped with drum and bells, looking like an upturned grand piano. A beautifully carved violin is said to have belonged to Charles II. You can hear recordings of the instruments in the gallery.

Look into the gallery opposite Costume Court to find out what artists like Leonardo and here, Raphael, meant by 'cartoon'. These Raphael Cartoons, huge as they are, were painted in 1515 as designs for tapestries for the Sistine Chapel in Rome. Charles I, then Prince of Wales, bought them in 1623, Queen Victoria lent them to the museum in 1865 and here they have remained.

The Great Bed of Ware

The Great Bed of Ware is in Room 52, among the series of period furnished rooms. This huge oak bed, made in England about 1580, is large enough to hold four couples. It is decorated at the bedhead with carvings of bearded men. The bed was once installed in an inn and (by custom) all those who slept in it carved their initials on it. It is mentioned by Sir Toby Belch in *Twelfth Night*. Oddly enough, four-poster beds were designed to give privacy in an age when many people lived, ate and slept in the same room. The Great Bed of Ware certainly defeated this object.

Royal relics

In Room 53, devoted to English embroidery between 1540 and 1640, is a military scarf said to have been worn by Charles I at the battle of Edgehill in 1642. The upholstered chair in this room, now faded but once bright red, is believed to have been used by the king at his trial in Westminster Hall.

There is another royal relic in Room 54—part of the hangings known as the Oxburgh Hangings, which were made by Mary, Queen of Scots, and Bess of Hardwick, Countess of Shrewsbury, about 1570, during the queen's captivity.

Room 55 contains the country's best collection of miniatures, including one of Anne of Cleves ('the Flemish mare' whom Henry VIII declined to live with) by Holbein, and many by the great Elizabethan miniaturist Nicholas Hilliard.

Arms and armour

The Victoria and Albert's examples of European arms and armour (in Rooms 88a and 90) have been selected specially to show the various techniques of ornament applied to swords, firearms, helmets, rapiers, hand daggers, breast plates and escutcheons. There are wheel-lock carbines inlaid with engraved staghorn; a 1520 steel escutcheon engraved with a crowned Polish eagle; flint-lock pistols with engraved and gilded mounts, and an air-gun said to have belonged to George II. This has a walnut stock mounted with cast and chiselled silver and inlaid with engraved silver.

The Pusey Horn legend

While on this floor, walk through the silver display in the corridor numbered (as you go from the Armoury) 69 to 65. This collection of Continental and English domestic silver is the finest in the world.

Amongst all the magnificence is the Pusey Horn (fifteenth century) to which is attached a legend dating back to Canute. There are many instances of odd land tenures in England. One such was said to concern Pusey in Oxfordshire. According to legend, Canute gave William Pusey the manor, and presented him with the Pusey Horn as a token of ownership. The horn is of ox or buffalo, mounted near the centre with a silver gilt band. It stands on two skinny legs attached to the band. In James II's reign, the manor was recovered in a lawsuit by the production of the Pusey Horn, which Judge Jeffreys (of the 'Bloody Assizes' fame) said he recognised as the genuine horn once presented by King Canute.

Saturday projects

A new scheme of Saturday projects for boys and girls has replaced the Victoria and Albert Afternoon Club. The excellent holiday lectures are open to all children. Write to the Education Dept., V. & A., London SW7 2RL.

Admission

Open weekdays except Fridays 10 a.m. to 5.40 p.m., Sundays 2.30 p.m. to 6 p.m. The museum is closed on Christmas Eve, Christmas Day and Boxing Day.

How to get there

The museum has two entrances. One is on the west side of the building in Exhibition Road, where there is also a subway leading to South Kensington underground station. But the main entrance is in Cromwell Road. Buses include Nos. 14, 30 and 74.

19. IMPERIAL WAR MUSEUM

Two massive 15-inch guns (from H.M.S. *Resolution* and *Ramillies)* guard the entrance to the Imperial War Museum. Each weighs 100 tons.

The Dam Buster
To the left and right off the main entrance hall are the small galleries, while the main exhibition is housed in the enormous lower floor down the steps in the centre.

The **Victoria and George Cross Room** is a good place to start, first gallery on the right, with stories of gallantry in war and mementoes of the heroes like 16-year-old John Cornwell, who guarded his gun to the death at the battle of Jutland and Guy Gibson, the Dam Buster. Further along is the **Documents Room** with fascinating items like the original German surrender document of 4th May 1945 and Hitler's political testament written shortly before his death. There are temporary displays in the other galleries on this side.

On the left of the stairs are the **Mountbatten Room** devoted to the family of distinguished sailors and more medals and decorations in the **Uniforms, Medals and Insignia Room,** including America's highest award for bravery won by General Douglas McArthur. The Imperial German Army must have looked very impressive to judge from the headgear shown here.

A pigeon parachute
Down the stairs, turning right you come to the first section of the new chronologically organised exhibition, **The Road to War** 1870-1914. The events leading to war are recorded in maps, charts, recruiting posters, weapons and uniforms. Tableaux show a troop train and a 1914 recruiting centre and the harsh life around the trenches. A sniper's hideout is represented and grenades, rations and equipment are displayed with items like a German man-trap and a pigeon parachute.

There are heavy guns like the 4.5 inch howitzer and the 60 pounder here, as well as the standard 18 pounder. Nearly 100 million rounds of ammunition were fired from 18 pounders between 1914 and 1918: that represents 43 rounds for every minute of the war.

Monty's caravans

'Old Bill', a red London bus, is the friendliest vehicle on display (among the tanks and jeeps), the last survivor of the troop-carrying B type buses used on the Western front. Field Marshal Montgomery's campaign caravans are the basis of a section on the Second World War. Two were captured from Italian generals in North Africa and the third was Leyland-built in 1944.

'Doodle bug'

The history of air warfare is covered by models of most aircraft used since 1914 as well as actual aircraft and sections of them, like the Sopwith Camel, probably the best British fighter of the First World War, and the Focke-Wulf FW 190, probably the best German fighter of the Second World War. The museum has one of the versatile de Havilland Mosquitoes and a Spitfire Mark I which probably destroyed at least five enemy aircraft in the Battle of Britain. A German flying bomb V1 or 'doodle bug' is here with part of its 160 ft launching ramp, as well as its successor the V2. The V2 had a maximum speed of 3,500 m.p.h. and a range of over 200 miles. More than 1,000 V2s fell on Britain between September 1944 and March 1945.

Apart from showing a history of most of our life and times, the Imperial War Museum contains a number of reference departments of outstanding importance, and a cinema that seats 210.

The **Film Library** holds nearly 25 million feet of film, including the Battle of the Somme, Desert Victory, Burma Victory, captured German newsreels showing their side of the war, and films on the work of the Royal Navy, the Royal Flying Corps and the R.A.F. Special film shows will be organised on request for parties from schools, colleges, cadet corps, etc. Three weeks' notice is requested. Escorted tours of the museum can also be arranged on request.

Films are normally shown in the cinema at 3 p.m. on Saturdays and Sundays. There are additional performances during the school holidays and on public holidays.

Admission

The Imperial War Museum is open from Monday to Saturday 10 a.m. to 5.50 p.m., Sundays 2 p.m. to 5.50 p.m. except Good Friday, Christmas Eve, Christmas Day, Boxing Day and New Year's Day.

How to get there

The museum is in Lambeth Road, London SE1, and the nearest Underground stations are Lambeth North and Elephant and Castle. Buses include nos. 3, 10, 44, 59, 109, 133, 155, 159, 172, 177 and 184.

Across the road from the entrance to the museum is a blue plaque marking the house in which Captain Bligh of the *Bounty* once lived. (It is always worth looking at the blue plaques. They commemorate famous people in many walks of life.)

20. BRITISH MUSEUM

The British Museum is one of the greatest treasure-houses in the world. It owes its beginning to Sir Hans Sloane, an Irishman who was born in 1660, the year Charles II was restored to the throne.

As a young man, Sloane studied botany, chemistry and anatomy, and later became the first physician to be made a hereditary baronet. He was one of the doctors who certified 'Queen Anne's dead!' in 1714.

Sloane had many scientific interests. He was president of the Royal Society in succession to Sir Isaac Newton, and had a fine collection of antiques, botanical specimens (some collected in Jamaica), gems and curiosities. He also had a library of more than 50,000 books and 4,000 manuscripts.

Only fifteen people at a time!

Sir Hans' valuable collection (offered for the low sum of £20,000), plus the presentation of the Royal Library of George III, persuaded Parliament to run a national lottery to raise funds to buy the Sloane collection and to administer a museum. A house was bought in Bloomsbury and the British Museum was opened in 1759 — to 15 people at a time, three days a week.

As the museum grew the building was added to and rebuilt. Today it is once again bursting at the seams, and a big rebuilding programme is under way.

The main entrance is in Great Russell Street.

There is so much to see the problem is where to begin. A map of the different galleries is helpful, and may be bought for 5p at the postcard counter in the main entrance, where there is also a direction board.

Past the postcards is the **Egyptian Sculpture Gallery,** where there are statues of kings and gods with heads of animals and birds, and a massive granite arm which probably came from a statue of Egypt's greatest king, Thothmoses III, who died about

1500 B.C. His head is on the staircase in the Front Hall. (On the Embankment is a 68 ft. monolith known as Cleopatra's Needle. This obelisk—which has no connection with Cleopatra—was erected by Thothmoses, and towed to England in a cylinder in Queen Victoria's reign.)

Before you explore the Egyptian Sculpture Gallery you might like to detour to the **Assyrian Saloon.** The entrance—on the immediate left as you walk towards the Egyptian exhibits—is guarded by two winged, human-headed monsters known as cherubims. Round the walls are acutely observed and vividly sculptured panels that once covered the walls of the palace of Assyrian kings. Some of the panels show a king in his chariot hunting lions. Other scenes show the Assyrian army besieging walled cities, using battering rams on wheels that look very much like modern tanks. Downstairs are glass cases showing some of the actual breast plates, shields, helmets and swords used in these battles. The stairway leads from the Assyrian Saloon, near a triumphant procession returning from a hunt with dead lions, birds and a hare.

Broken by a madman

The Assyrian exhibits lead to two more cherubims, each weighing about seven tons, and to a sort of 'crossroads'. Directly in front is a Roman mosaic laid in France in the second century A.D. Looking down at the mosaic is the crouching Aphrodite, sculptured about 250 B.C., lent to the museum by the Queen. Straight ahead is a statue of Apollo playing a lute. In the rooms behind him are early Roman wall paintings, tiny bronze figures, jewellery, and the **Portland Vase.** This lovely vase is made of two layers of glass: white on dark blue, the white being cut away like a cameo to show the design in relief. The vase is now made up of fragments. It was broken by a madman in 1845, but skilfully put together again.

If you turn left at the Roman mosaic pavement, you walk through to the Duveen Gallery, where the **Elgin Marbles** are displayed. These friezes and statues from the Parthenon in Athens are called after Lord Elgin, who collected them in Athens in 1801-1803. He brought them to England, and sold them to the government for £35,000, about half what they cost him to collect and ship. You can hire a half-hour sound guide (12½p) on the Elgin Marbles, which are amongst the greatest sculptures of the world. Most of them were carved between 447 and 432 B.C., and show vigorous riders and horses, bulls, and girls with sacrificial vessels.

Mummies of cats and kittens

Return to the Egyptian Sculpture Gallery. A staircase at the left-hand end (lined with framed mosaics of horses, fish, sea creatures and hunting scenes) leads to the **2nd Egyptian Room.**

Here are Egyptian mummies and their intricately carved mummy cases. Among them is the body of a pre-dynastic man (with hair breaking through his cracked skin) who died some 3,500 years before the birth of Christ. His body was preserved by the hot sands of Egypt under which he was buried. He is lying just as he was found in his grave.

Leading out of the 2nd Egyptian Room is the **1st Egyptian Room,** where there are various bodies showing the great skill and care taken in wrapping them in bandages after death. There are also mummies of cats and kittens, a gazelle, a jackal and a dog.

A hungry hippopotamus

On the walls of the 1st Egyptian Room are paintings copied exactly from the Egyptian tombs. One picture shows a man being judged after death. His heart (which the Egyptians equated with the soul) is being weighed on a pair of scales and balanced against a feather, the symbol of truth and justice. Nearby stands a hippopotamus, eager to eat the man if he fails the test. (If he passes he will live 'happily ever after' in the beautiful Land of the West.)

As you come out of the 2nd Egyptian Room turn left and walk through the Room of Writing (on stone) to the staircase guarded by a three-storey high 'top-hatted' totem pole from British Columbia. At the foot of the staircase turn into the museum's stamp collection, where there are cabinets holding stamps from all over the world.

The stamp collection leads to the **King's Library,** another of the museum's great treasures. Here thousands of books, many of them unique, are kept, including Caxton's *Aesop's Fables,* printed in Westminster in 1484, the first folio of *Mr. William Shakespeare's Comedies, Histories and Tragedies,* printed in London in 1623, and the Gutenberg 42-lines-to-the-page Bible, the first substantial book printed in moveable type.

Scott's last message

Straight ahead is the **Manuscript Saloon,** where there are letters and documents written by famous people, including the diary of Scott of the Antarctic, showing the page on which his last poignant message was written in pencil: 'For God's sake look after our people'. There is an essay written by Edward VI showing corrections made by his tutor; the original manuscript of *Alice's Adventures Under Ground* (as *Alice in Wonderland* was first called by Lewis Carroll) with illustrations by the author; and a letter from Nelson to his 'dearest Emma', Lady Hamilton, written two days before the battle of Trafalgar. Here, too, there is always someone looking at a copy of Magna Carta.

The **Clock Room** is well worth a visit. Outstanding here are a large fourteenth century iron clock—still clicking away the minutes—and a carillon clock made in 1598 by Nicholas Vallin, clockmaker to Elizabeth I.

The British Museum often changes its exhibits, so visitors wanting to see something in particular should make enquiries first.

Admission

Open Monday to Saturday 10 a.m. to 5 p.m., Sundays 2.30 p.m. to 6 p.m. The museum is not open on Christmas Eve, Christmas Day, Boxing Day or Good Friday.

How to get there

The nearest underground stations are Tottenham Court Road and Holborn (Kingsway). Useful buses include Nos. 8, 14, 24, 25, 29 and 73.

---

21. POLLOCK'S TOY THEATRE AND TOY MUSEUM

Peep shows with eye-holes thoughtfully provided at different levels are among the joys of Pollock's Toy Theatre and Toy Museum, which occupies two little houses joined together.

The founder was Benjamin Pollock, who married the daughter of John Redington, a printer of play books—containing the script, characters and scenery for toy theatre plays. The toy theatre was something more than a toy, being a real theatre in miniature, with all its plays adapted from real productions that had been staged in London theatres.

In 1873 Pollock took over his father-in-law's business in Hoxton. He did all the prints himself, and when his two daughters grew up they painted those set aside for painting. It was these plain and tinted prints that inspired Robert Louis Stevenson's famous description: 'Penny plain and tuppence coloured'. (A battered wax Benjamin Pollock is sitting in the window of the museum—caught in the very act of printing one of his lithos of an actor.)

Pollock's incorporates a toy shop. Downstairs the walls are covered with calico printed with 'Little Liz' dolls (in mop caps). Round about are various theatres already assembled. Up the stairways are framed old jig-saw puzzles and jumping-jacks, shabby puppets, a tiny grocer's shop with far-too-large miniature cans of Huntley and Palmer's ginger nuts and Bird's custard, and dozens of the dolls that Victorian children loved.

The dolls may appeal most to the girls, but boys share their enthusiasm for toy theatres. More and more are sold every year, and boys who do buy them are following in famous footsteps, as Sir Winston Churchill had one as a boy.

Admission

Open every weekday 10 a.m. to 5 p.m. Entrance is by contribution, with a minimum of 20p for adults and 10p for children. School parties by arrangement. Telephone 01-636 3452 for details.

How to get there

Pollock's Toy Museum is just off Tottenham Court Road, at the back of Goodge Street Underground station. Buses going near include Nos. 14, 24 and 73.

22. MADAME TUSSAUD'S

Everybody enjoys Madame Tussaud's, in Marylebone Road, and the possibility of staring intently at a wax figure who turns out to be real, or vice versa. There are usually about 450 figures on show, with frequent changes. The pinnacle of success has been reached when one's model is placed in Madame Tussaud's.

Modelling victims of the guillotine

Madame Tussaud herself, 81 years old, and black bonneted, welcomes you to the exhibition. This self-portrait was her last. Marie was born in Strasbourg, but brought up in Paris by an uncle, Philippe Curtius, a doctor who had his own waxworks. He taught Marie wax modelling, and she made her earliest surviving portrait, of Voltaire, when she was 17.

In 1780 Marie went to the Court of Versailles as tutor in wax modelling to Louis XVI's sister Elizabeth. So, when the Revolution broke out, she was imprisoned as a royalist, and only her skill in modelling saved her from the guillotine, the blade of which is now in the Chamber of Horrors, along with the death masks of Louis XVI and Marie Antoinette, which Marie was forced to make. Models of the nobility were needed by the Revolutionaries for propaganda, and the head of almost every distinguished victim was modelled either by Marie or her uncle (plate 7).

After marrying (and leaving) Francois Tussaud, Marie came to England in 1802 with about 30 of her best models. For 33 years she toured the country with her two sons, setting up her figures in halls and theatres, and making new models.

At last, in 1835, tired of travelling, Madame Tussaud opened her exhibition permanently in London.

The Conservatory and Heroes

The Conservatory features portrait figures in wax of people in all walks of life, including Kevin Keegan, the international footballer, Glenda Jackson, Lisa Minelli and Len Murray. And as it is a Conservatory, Percy Thrower, the well-known gardener, is there, as well as Richard Burton, millionaire Paul Getty and conductor Andre Previn. Among the heroes you will find Rudolf Nureyev, Muhammad Ali, Kojak and two old favourites who never lose their appeal for parents, Humphrey Bogart and Marilyn Monroe.

These portrait figures are presented with sequences of changing lights and sounds.

The Grand Hall

The reigning sovereign has always been given a place of honour in the exhibition. Queen Elizabeth II (like all monarchs since George III) gave a sitting to the waxwork's sculptor, and stands regally wearing Garter robes. Prince Charles is wearing a replica of the uniform he wore at his investiture as Prince of Wales. Both uniforms were made simultaneously, and only Madame Tussaud's, apart from the Royal Family (and the tailor!) knew what he was going to wear.

This magnificent hall is thronged with famous people—Queen Elizabeth and many other kings and queens of England, Shakespeare with Dickens and Sir Walter Scott; Sir Winston Churchill and Lloyd George; Pablo Picasso and Henry Moore, and Mrs. Margaret Thatcher, the first woman to become a party leader in Britain.

George Washington (modelled by Madame Tussaud) stands with other American presidents, including Abraham Lincoln and Jimmy Carter. Henry VIII is there with his six wives, and there is a group all modelled by Madame Tussaud — Voltaire, and Louis XVI, Marie Antoinette and their two young children, Madame Elizabeth and the Dauphin.

British politicians glare at one another, and Pope John XXIII and Pope Paul VI smile benignly.

The Chamber of Horrors

In this gloomy chamber, popular with children but not with the over-sensitive adult, are men and women set apart by evil, or by the evil that has befallen them—from Robespierre and Crippen to Lee Harvey Oswald (who assassinated President Kennedy, who is standing in the Grand Hall).

The Tableaux

The tableaux are among the most popular of the exhibits, showing in all too life-like accuracy the murder of the Princes in the Tower and the execution of Mary, Queen of Scots in the hall of Fotheringhay Castle. But here too is the 'Sleeping Beauty'—in reality a portrait of Madame du Barry by Dr. Curtius. It is the oldest figure in the exhibition.

Another great favourite among the tableaux is a reconstruction of the famous picture, by Victorian artist W. J. Eames, of a small Royalist being interrogated by Cromwellians, called 'When Did You Last See Your Father?' And there, too, is the Duke of Wellington studying the death mask of his old enemy, Napoleon, as he often did in real life.

The Battle of Trafalgar

A hero of yesterday who has never lost appeal is Lord Nelson, and the spectacle of 'The Battle of Trafalgar ... as it happened' draws great crowds, and is especially popular with boys. To recreate the decks of Nelson's flagship *Victory* cost over £50,000—more than the ship itself.

The spectacle is dominated by the noise of cannon fire, sounding just as it did as Nelson's fleet approached the French and Spanish fleets. The battle is played out on an exact reproduction of the lower gun deck: guns, crew, equipment stripped for action amid the smoke and smell of battle, and above and around, in a sequence of light and sound, cannons fire, masts fall, ships collide and boarders are repulsed. (Recordings for the spectacle were made aboard *Victory* and on *Foudroyant*, the oldest warship still afloat, in Portsmouth Harbour.)

After watching and listening to the battle, pass down to the orlop deck, below the waterline, where Nelson is dying.

Admission

Open every day of the year except Christmas Day. On weekdays, between April and September 10 a.m. to 6.30 p.m. The rest of the year 10 a.m. to 5.30 p.m. On Saturdays and Sundays 10 a.m. to 6.30 p.m. Admission charge.

Madame Tussaud's also runs the London Planetarium, which is next door, and you can buy a combined ticket.

For party bookings, contact the Party Booking Office, Madame Tussaud's and the London Planetarium, Marylebone Road, London, NW1 (01-486 1121 or 01-935 6861). Parties over 20 qualify for a reduction.

23. THE LONDON PLANETARIUM

The London Planetarium performances take place at regular intervals, so if you want to see both the stars and the waxworks, it may suit you to go into the Planetarium first. Here, under the green copper dome, you can study the universe of stars, with an astronomer for a guide.

This man-made universe is produced by a complicated, massive almost creature-like £100,000 Zeiss projector. It contains some 29,000 separate parts of 200 optical projectors. It is 13ft. high and weighs more than 2 tons. There are projectors for the Sun, the Moon, and the five 'naked-eye' planets—Mercury, Venus, Mars, Jupiter and Saturn—and between them two 'star carriers' project 8,900 stars, correctly spaced, correctly graduated in brightness.

At the beginning of this century, it was realised that a mechanical model of the heavens was impracticable. No model could be made to a workable scale. For instance, if the Sun were represented by a two-foot globe, the Earth (200 ft. away) would be the size of a pea. The problem of reproducing the heavens was solved in 1918 by Dr. Bauresfeld, of the optical firm of Carl Zeiss, of Jena. But his instrument, remarkable as it was, showed only the stars in the Northern Hemisphere. Since that first machine, additions and technical improvements have been introduced, and the instrument in the London Planetarium incorporates all these. It was manufactured by the Zeiss company in West Germany and can show the position of the stars and planets as they appear from any place on earth, at any moment in time from 50 years before the birth of Christ to some 2,000 years into the future.

Admission

The Planetarium is open all the year round (except Christmas Day), daily 11 a.m. to 6 p.m. (or to 4.30 p.m. from December to Easter). Admission charge (also combined rate with Madame Tussaud's). On most weekdays in term time the 11 a.m. and 2 p.m. presentations are given specially for schoolchildren and those taking the Nuffield Physics course.

How to get there

Madame Tussaud's and the Planetarium are next door to one another in Marylebone Road. The easiest way to get there is to go to Baker Street station by Underground, or by one of the many buses passing nearby: Nos. 2, 13, 18, 27, 30, 59, 74, 113 and 159.

Dickens lovers may like to cross the road after coming out of Madame Tussaud's. Just past the church of St. Marylebone (where Robert and Elizabeth Browning were married) is Devonshire Terrace. Ferguson House, on the corner, replaces No. 1 Devonshire Terrace, where Dickens lived from 1839 to 1851.

While there he wrote several of his most famous books, including *The Old Curiosity Shop, Dombey and Son* and *David Copperfield*. By the entrance is a mural showing Dickens and some of his best known characters.

24. LONDON'S PARKS

Did you know that you can walk in parkland almost all the way from Trafalgar Square to Kensington Palace? Here is the route. Cross under Admiralty Arch, and skirt the Mall by walking along St. James's Park towards Buckingham Palace. Then cross into Green Park, heading towards Hyde Park Corner. Cross into Hyde Park, and you can walk through its broad acres, and through Kensington Gardens right up to Kensington Palace.

For playing 'paille maille'

Most Londoners prefer the 93 acres of **St. James's Park** to all others. It has a charming five-acre lake, pelicans, and is a sanctuary for migratory birds. There are fine views of Buckingham Palace and Whitehall too!

It was not laid out as a park until Charles II employed Le Notre, who had planned the gardens at Versailles. Le Notre drew up plans for a lake and islands, an aviary along Birdcage Walk, and a 600-yard course where Charles and his favourites could play the old French game of *paille maille.*

No one plays *paille maille* here any more, but the game gave its name to Pall Mall.

A favourite place for duels

Green Park is still an informal park covering 53 acres and is beautiful all the year round, particularly in the spring, when crocuses and daffodils are out. It was once a favourite place for duels. As you walk through it look for the fardel rest in the Piccadilly pavement as you approach Hyde Park. This high bench was erected many years ago so that porters could rest their bundles, or fardels, there before toiling up the hill.

The traffic roars round Hyde Park Corner with such ferocity it is best to take the underpass and arrive in **Hyde Park** safely.

Wolves and hangings

Wolves once lived here and were such a menace to travellers they were ruthlessly hunted down by the Saxon kings. At one time, the land belonged to the monks of Westminster Abbey, but at the Dissolution of the Monasteries, Henry VIII enclosed the park and declared it royal property. He stocked it with deer, and he and his daughter Elizabeth hunted there.

Charles I opened the park to the public, and Cromwell reviewed his troops there. He had an undignified experience while driving a coach and six. The horses got out of control, and Cromwell was 'flung out of the coachbox upon the pole' and was carried along for some distance with his feet trailing on the ground. When Charles II was restored to the throne, Cromwell and other Parliamentarians who were buried in Westminster Abbey were disinterred and hanged in ignomiy at Tyburn. A plaque set into the road near Marble Arch marks the site of this terrible three-sided gallows. Numbers of people could be hanged at the same time, and a hanging was one of the popular spectacles of the day, with hawkers selling gingerbread and generally making a holiday of the occasion.

Charles II made Hyde Park the centre of fashion, but by William III's reign it had become dangerous with footpads. When he went to live at Kensington Palace (because the country air was better for his asthma), he had Hyde Park hung with 300 lamps to make his journeys safer. The lighted roadway that William used became known as La Route du Roi—the origin (probably) of Rotten Row.

The Serpentine, a lovely lake of 40 acres, well-stocked with waterfowl, was made at the request of Queen Caroline, George II's wife. She created Kensington Gardens (where its share of the Serpentine is called the Long Water) by enclosing 300 acres of Hyde Park. She wanted to enclose that too, and St. James's Park. But when she enquired the likely cost, Prime Minister Walpole replied severely: "Three crowns, Madam—England, Scotland and Ireland!"

A notorious duel

In George III's reign Hyde Park became notorious for duelling, 172 duels being fought there during his reign. The most famous was between the bad Lord Mohun, and James Douglas, 4th Duke of Hamilton. Each man killed the other. In a letter telling of the duel, Dean Swift wrote: "The dog Mohun was killed on the spot, but while the duke was over him, Mohun shortened his sword, and stabbed him in the shoulder to the heart. The duke died on the grass, before he could reach his house, and was brought home in his coach".

A miscalculation

Marble Arch was designed by John Nash (died 1835), who also laid out Regent's Park. With the Marble Arch, however, he made a miscalculation. The original plan was to make the arch a spectacular main entrance to Buckingham Palace—but it was just a few inches too narrow for the State coach to go through. It was set up in Hyde Park in 1851.

Colourful occasions

Today Hyde Park covers 360 acres and is a place for picnics, for sleeping in the sun, or for listening to cranks and prophets at Speakers' Corner.

Royal Salutes (of 41 guns) are fired in Hyde Park on special occasions such as the Queen's real birthday (April 21st), her 'official' birthday (on a Saturday in June), the anniversary of her Accession (February 6th), the Coronation anniversary (June 2nd), the Duke of Edinburgh's birthday (June 10th) and the Queen Mother's birthday (August 4th) (plate 9).

Another big occasion for Hyde Park is the **Veteran Car Run,** held from Hyde Park to Brighton on the first Sunday in November. The veterans must have been manufactured between 1895 and 1904. The annual run is held in memory of the 'Emancipation Day' run to Brighton in November 1896—to celebrate the lifting of the law which laid down that vehicles on a highway must not travel faster than 4 m.p.h. and must be preceded by a man walking ahead.

Peter Pan's garden

Kensington Palace was remodelled by Christopher Wren for William III in 1689—and till the death of George II in 1760 it was the official residence of the reigning monarch. Queen Victoria was born there in 1819—and lived there till her accession in 1837. Victoria was described as a child as 'a pretty little princess, plump as a partridge'—and she spent many hours playing in **Kensington Gardens,** which cover over 270 acres. It is still a favourite park for children. First of all there is the statue of **Peter Pan,** near the Long Water. On the pedestal beneath him are fairies, rabbits and field mice, whose wings and ears have been polished over the years by the constant fondling of small caressing hands. The statue was erected in 1912 (plate 11).

Another favourite place in Kensington Gardens is the **Round Pond,** enjoyed equally by swans, dogs, children and adults. It is a great place for sailing boats or flying kites.

Leaving the Round Pond behind you, walk to the right up the Broad Walk. On the left, near Bayswater, there is a playground of see-saws and swings—and an **Elfin Oak,** now enclosed by a protective railing. It was carved in 1930 by Ivor Innes from an old stump from Richmond Park. The tree was restored in 1966 and a tiny plaque gives credit for the work to the fairies. (They had some help, however, from Spike Milligan, the actor.)

Kensington Gardens is popular with very small children and their nannies and also with gardeners, as there are flowers in bloom almost all the year, and trees, in great abundance and beauty. Many elms were declared dangerous and cut down some years ago. They had been planted under the direction of Queen Caroline. According to legend, they were planted to match the disposition of the Guards at the battle of Blenheim, when John Churchill, Duke of Marlborough, led his troops (in person) and scored a victory against the French in 1704.

Tournaments and jousts

London's other great park is quite separate from St James's, Green Park, Hyde Park and Kensington Gardens. It is **Regent's Park**, roughly circular and covering 472 acres. It includes the London Zoo. It was once one of the royal hunting parks and has always been well looked after. A mound was built round it in the early days to keep deer in and poachers out, and lodges were built for the gamekeepers, who were paid fourpence a day.

In Charles II's reign about 1,000 trees in the park (always predominantly oak, ash, elm, whitethorn and maple), were cut down to build frigates for the navy.

Regent's Park as we know it was laid out by Nash for the Prince Regent. The favourite entrance is the Clarence Gate entrance from Baker Street, as it is so near transport and is the quickest way to the ducks.

Tournaments and joustings were often held in Regent's Park in honour of Queen Elizabeth. One tournament led to a famous quarrel between the young Earl of Essex and Sir Charles Blount, another courtier and a handsome man who caught Elizabeth's eye. He fought with such a dash and gaiety that Elizabeth rewarded him by presenting him with a gold and enamel chess queen. Blount tied the gift to his arm with a piece of scarlet ribbon. The jealous Essex said scornfully: "Now I perceive that every fool must have a favour!" Sir Charles challenged the queen's favourite to a duel, and wounded him in the thigh, but Elizabeth refused to allow the two young men to continue their quarrel, and afterwards they became close friends.

Among the attractions of Regent's Park are the lake covering 22 acres, where one can hire rowing boats, the rose garden (called Queen Mary's Garden as a tribute to her life-long interest in the park and its flower gardens) and the Open Air Theatre, where in the summer Shakespearean and other plays are performed. It is a magical setting for *A Midsummer Night's Dream,* though it is a good idea to take a rug: it can grow chilly, and the midges bite unprotected legs.

On Easter Monday the annual **London Harness Horse Parade** is held in the Inner Circle of Regent's Park. Judging takes place between 10 a.m. and noon.

25. LONDON ZOO

Giraffes, which look like sedately animated jig-saw puzzles, have to splay their legs out when they want to drink. They are the tallest animals in the world, averaging about 15 ft., but they have only seven joints in their long necks.

Sparrows, on the other hand, have 14 joints in their short necks.

To keep 'in the pink', flamingoes need a special diet. Without it, their feathers would grow white.

Saved-up pocket money can be very well spent buying the *London Zoo Guide*. It tells you about all the creatures in the zoo—*and* it contains an excellent map.

Choose a fine day (if you can) for your visit to London Zoo. Pack a lunch (though there are many cafeterias and kiosks there) and set off *without* any food for the inhabitants. They are very adequately fed and to keep healthy they must keep to their diet. Besides, if animals learn to beg, they become so greedy that they will eat *anything* — coats, handbags, gloves — even cameras. They may also try to eat you.

The zoo's family usually numbers between 6,800 and 7,000 animals, fish, reptiles and birds. (No one bothers to count the insects.) It covers 36 acres, and the 'resident' quarters and the gardens are constantly being altered and improved. The magnificent new lion terraces, opened by the Queen in 1976 are the latest popular attraction.

The most valuable and popular mammals in the zoo are Ching-Ching and Chia-Chia, the giant pandas presented to the British people by the Chinese Government in 1974. Ching-Ching ('Crystal Bright') is the female. The name of the male, Chia-Chia (pronounced Cha-Cha), means 'Most Excellent'. They are great friends and spend hours playing together, or splashing about in their bath tub.

Their food includes bamboo shoots, and a delicious steamed 'porridge' made from rice, maize meal, milk, eggs, bean cake, sugar, bone meal, salt and trace elements.

There are very few giant pandas in captivity—two in Washington, one in Paris, two in Tokyo, one in North Korea, and about 50 in Chinese zoos, and naturalists who know the bamboo jungles of China estimate that there are probably not more than 250 left in the wild. Wild pandas are thought to live mostly on bamboo shoots, and through this habit they have evolved an elongated bone sticking out of the wrist. This can be held against the five normal claws when grabbing hold of the bamboo.

The most popular animals, the apes and monkeys, are housed in the new Michael Sobell Pavilions, where they live in family groups or as colonies. Visitors watch from covered walkways.

Elephants and rhinos already have a new pavilion. The Snowdon Aviary, opened in 1965, is the zoo's first out-of-doors walk-through aviary. With its pools and waterfalls, it houses over 140 birds, including herons, egrets, ibises, kestrels and spoonbills. More new aviaries are planned. So is a new children's zoo—and a new house for invertebrates.

Housekeeping for the zoo family is expensive; it costs over £120,000 a year. Some of the regular items on the shopping list are 300 tons of hay and clover, 45 tons of meat, 40,000 eggs, 22,000 pints of milk, 80 tons of carrots, 45 tons of potatoes, 27 tons of cabbage, as well as oranges, grapes, earth-worms, maggots, melons and jam.

Some of the residents do present food problems—the pink-feathered birds such as flamingoes and scarlet ibises, for instance. They can live perfectly healthily on quite ordinary foods, but unless their diet includes pink chemicals called carotenoids they cannot grow pink feathers. To stop them turning white, these birds at London Zoo are given cockles and shrimps, both of which are rich in carotenoids.

Finding enough ants for the ant-eaters would be difficult, but they thrive on a substitute diet of raw minced meat with milk and raw eggs. To keep reindeer in good condition, they need some of their natural food, a lichen called 'reindeer moss' which is specially imported. So is sugar from West Africa—a treat for the elephants, which each eat over 130 lb. of food daily, including hay, oats, biscuits, carrots, potatoes, cabbages, fresh and dried fruit and cod liver oil.

One of the most delightful sections of the zoo is the 'moonlight world' in the basement of the Charles Clore Pavilion for Mammals. Here, day and night have been reversed, so we can see nocturnal animals such as badgers going about their nightly activities. (Normally, during the day, they would be curled up and invisible in their sleeping boxes.) Other animals in this special world include kinkajous, bush babies, flying squirrels, and hamsters and gerbils in cut-away, glass-fronted burrows that let us watch their private lives, including the feeding and rearing of their young.

Do not miss the Children's Zoo Farm, where you meet at close quarters all sorts of animals that make good pets, and where *small* children can have rides on tiny Shetland ponies or diminutive donkeys. The Children's Zoo Farm is open all year round. It opens at 10.30 a.m. and a notice of the closing time is posted on the gate. The rides take place in the summer from 11.30 a.m. till noon, and from 1.15 p.m. till 4 p.m. (but not when it is wet and not on Sundays).

Children of any age can feel like explorers and ride a camel, or ride in a trap drawn by a llama—from 1.45 p.m. till 3.45 p.m.—from Easter to October (but not when it is wet and not on Sundays).

Feeding times

If you study the 'You are Here' maps round the zoo, and the feeding timetables, you will be able to plan your day around several mealtimes. But remember that the lions (to keep them in good health) are not fed *at all* on Wednesdays, and the reptiles are fed *only* on Fridays, at 2.30 p.m. in the Reptile House.

Young people from nine to 18 can join the XYZ Club, the Young Zoologists' Club, based on London Zoo and Whipsnade Park. There are many privileges for members, including six free tickets a year, a membership badge, three copies a year of *The Zoo Magazine,* use of the free Information Bureau, painting and photographic competitions, film shows and lectures. If you want to know more, write to the XYZ Club, London Zoo, Regent's Park, London, N.W.1.

How to get there

London Zoo is a fair walk from Regent's Park underground station. Better to go to Baker Street station, and catch a No. 74 bus. This will take you to North Gate. (This bus comes from Knightsbridge, Hyde Park Corner and Marble Arch.) Alternatively, catch a No. 3 or No. 53 from Trafalgar Square, Piccadilly Circus or Regent Street. These buses will take you to Albany Street, within five minutes walk of the Main or South Gates.

To avoid disappointment note that feeding times, prices of admission, etc, have to be changed periodically. You can always check by ringing 01-722 3333.

A useful telephone number to know is that of the London Tourist Board, 26 Grosvenor Gardens, London SW1—01-730 0791.

The publishers have made every effort to ensure the accuracy of the information in this book, but times of opening in particular are liable to alteration and intending visitors are advised to check with the London Tourist Board before setting out.